CLEVER Lili

40

STUDY GUIDE

China: Conflict, Crisis and Change, 1900–89

Edexcel - IGCSE

app available

www.GCSEHistory.com

CLEVER Lili

Published by Clever Lili Limited.

contact@cleverlili.com

First published 2020

ISBN 978-1-913887-39-1

Copyright notice

All rights reserved. No part of this publication may be reproduced in any form or by any means (including photocopying or storing it in any medium by electronic means and whether or not transiently or incidentally to some other use of this publication) with the written permission of the copyright owner. Applications for the copyright owner's written permission should be addressed to the publisher.

Clever Lili has made every effort to contact copyright holders for permission for the use of copyright material. We will be happy, upon notification, to rectify any errors or omissions and include any appropriate rectifications in future editions.

Cover by: PublicDomainPictures on Pixabay

Icons by: flaticon and freepik

Contributors: Jordan Hobbis, Jonathan Boyd, Shahan Abu Shumel Haydar

Edited by Paul Connolly and Rebecca Parsley

Design by Evgeni Veskov and Will Fox

All rights reserved

www.GCSEHistory.com

DISCOVER MORE OF OUR IGCSE HISTORY STUDY GUIDES
GCSEHistory.com and Clever Lili

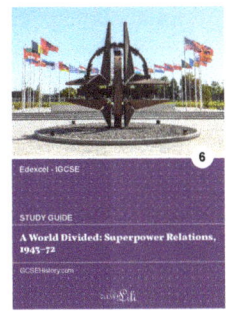

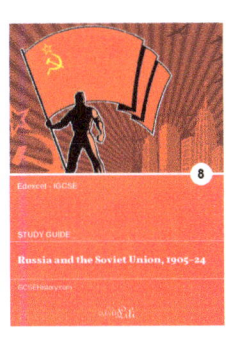

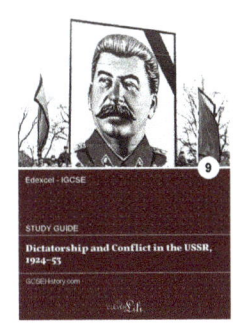

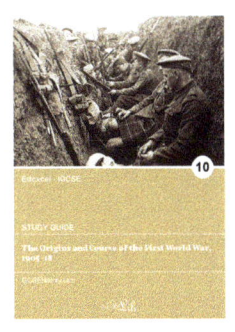

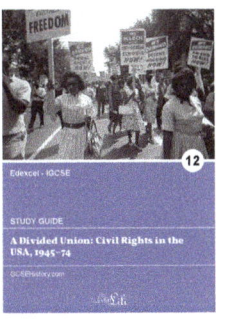

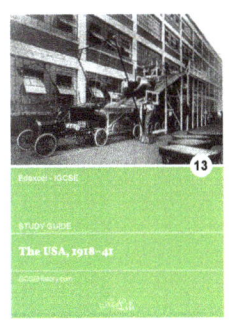

- 4: Germany: Development of Dictatorship, 1918-45
- 6: A World Divided: Superpower Relations, 1943-72
- 8: Russia and the Soviet Union, 1905-24
- 9: Dictatorship and Conflict in the USSR, 1924-53
- 10: The Origins and Course of the First World War, 1905-18
- 11: The Vietnam Conflict, 1945-75
- 12: A Divided Union: Civil Rights in the USA, 1945-74
- 13: The USA, 1918-41
- 16: Changes in Medicine, c1848-c1948

THE GUIDES ARE EVEN BETTER WITH OUR GCSE/IGCSE HISTORY WEBSITE APP AND MOBILE APP

GCSE History is a text and voice web and mobile app that allows you to easily revise for your GCSE/IGCSE exams wherever you are - it's like having your own personal GCSE history tutor. Whether you're at home or on the bus, GCSE History provides you with thousands of convenient bite-sized facts to help you pass your exams with flying colours. We cover all topics - with more than 120,000 questions - across the Edexcel, AQA and CIE exam boards.

GCSEHistory.com — GET IT ON Google Play — Download on the App Store

Contents

How to use this book.. 5

What is this book about?... 6

Revision suggestions... 8

Timelines

China: Conflict, Crisis and Change, 1900-89................................ 12

The Fall of the Qing, Warlordism and Chaos, 1900–34

China in 1900.. 14

Ruling in the Country.. 14

The Boxer Uprising... 15

Self-Strengthening Reform, 1902-11... 16

The 1911 Revolution.. 17

The Era of the Warlords, 1916-27.. 18

The May Fourth Movement, 1919.. 19

Sun Yat-Sen... 20

Chiang Kai-Shek.. 21

Guomindang.. 22

The Emergence of the Chinese Communist Party........................ 22

The Establishment of the United Front....................................... 23

The Northern Expedition... 24

The Shanghai Massacres.. 25

The Extermination Campaigns... 26

Manchuria, 1931.. 27

The Triumph of Mao and the CCP, 1934-49

The Jiangxi Soviet... 27

The Long March.. 29

Zunyi, 1935.. 30

Mao Zedong.. 31

Life at Yanan... 32

Xian Incident, 1936... 34

Japanese Invasion of China, 1937... 35

The War With Japan, 1937-45.. 36

The Civil War, 1946-49... 38

The Battle of Huaihai.. 39

Change Under Mao, 1949-63

Agrarian Reform Law, 1950.. 40

Marriage Law, 1950... 41

The Collectivisation of Agriculture... 42

The First Five Year Plan, 1952-57.. 43

The Great Leap Forward, 1958-62.. 43

The Great Famine, 1958-62... 45

Changes in the Role of Women... 45

Political Changes Under Mao.. 47

Mao Zedong Thought... 47

Thought Reform... 48

The Three-Anti Campaign, 1951.. 49

The Five-Anti Campaign, 1952.. 49

The Hundred Flowers Campaign, 1957...................................... 50

Sino-Soviet Relations, 1949-62.. 51

The Cultural Revolution and Its Impact, 1965-76

The Sino-Soviet Split... 52

The Cultural Revolution.. 53

The 'Up to the Mountains and Down to the Mountains' Campaign........... 55

China, 1976-89

The Gang of Four.. 56

Deng Xiaoping.. 57

Economic Change Under Deng Xiaoping.................................... 58

Birth Control... 59

Political Change Under Deng... 60

The Democracy Wall Movement... 61

Tiananmen Square... 62

Glossary... 64

Index.. 67

Quizzes, amazing exam preparation tools and more at GCSEHistory.com

HOW TO USE THIS BOOK

In this study guide, you will see a series of icons, highlighted words and page references. The key below will help you quickly establish what these mean and where to go for more information.

Icons

WHAT questions cover the key events and themes.

WHO questions cover the key people involved.

WHEN questions cover the timings of key events.

WHERE questions cover the locations of key moments.

WHY questions cover the reasons behind key events.

HOW questions take a closer look at the way in which events, situations and trends occur.

IMPORTANCE questions take a closer look at the significance of events, situations, and recurrent trends and themes.

DECISIONS questions take a closer look at choices made at events and situations during this era.

Highlighted words

Abdicate - occasionally, you will see certain words highlighted within an answer. This means that, if you need it, you'll find an explanation of the word or phrase in the glossary which starts on **page 64**.

Page references

Tudor *(p.7)* - occasionally, a certain subject within an answer is covered in more depth on a different page. If you'd like to learn more about it, you can go directly to the page indicated.

Get our free app at GCSEHistory.com

WHAT IS THIS BOOK ABOUT?

The China: Conflict, Crisis and Change, 1900-89 course investigates the major changes in China during the 20th century. The course focuses on the causes, course and consequences of the crucial events during this period, and you will study the different political, economic and military changes that occurred.

Purpose
This study guide will help you understand the complexities of 20th century China. You will investigate themes such as civil conflict, external influences on China, economic transformation, social transformation and the role of leadership. This guide will enable you to develop the historical thinking skills of causation and consequence, similarity and difference, and change and continuity.

Topics
This study guide is split into five key topic areas.
- The fall of the Qing, Warlordism and chaos, 1900-34.
- The triumph of Mao and the CCP, 1934-49.
- Change under Mao, 1949-64.
- The Cultural Revolution and its impact, 1965-76.
- China, 1976-89.

Key Individuals
Some of the key individuals studied on this course include:
- Empress Dowager Cixi.
- Sun Yat-sen.
- Chiang Kai-shek.
- Mao Zedong.
- Jiang Qing.
- Deng Xiaoping.

Key Events
Some of the key events and developments you will study on this course include:
- The Boxer Uprising.
- The 1911 Revolution.
- China under the Warlords.
- The development of the United Front.
- The Long March.
- War with Japan.
- Civil War.
- The Great Famine.
- The Great Leap Forward.
- The Hundred Flowers Campaign.
- The Cultural Revolution and its impact, 1965-76.
- Tiananmen Square.

Assessment
China: Conflict, Crisis and Change, 1900-89 topic forms the second half of paper two. You will have a total of 1 hour and 30 minutes to complete the paper. You should spend 45 minutes on the China: Conflict, Crisis and Change, 1900-89 section of the paper. There will be 3 exam questions which will assess what you have learned on the China 1900-89 course.

- Question a is worth 6 marks and asks you to explain two differences or similarities across the time period. You must use specific details from each example to fully explain the similarities or differences.
- Question b is worth 8 marks and asks you to explain two causes of an event. You must use accurate, relevant and detailed historical facts to show how each cause led to the event, or how each consequence resulted from it.

WHAT IS THIS BOOK ABOUT?

- Question c is worth 16 marks, and gives you a choice of one of two questions. It will ask you to make a judgement about 'how far' a historical statement is true. You must select at least three points to support your answer, use accurate, relevant and detailed knowledge to explain and analyse whether they support the statement, and reach a judgement based on the points that you have made. The question will give you two bullet points to help you answer, but you must use at least one more of your own.

REVISION SUGGESTIONS

Revision! A dreaded word. Everyone knows it's coming, everyone knows how much it helps with your exam performance, and everyone struggles to get started! We know you want to do the best you can in your IGCSEs, but schools aren't always clear on the best way to revise. This can leave students wondering:

- ✔ How should I plan my revision time?
- ✔ How can I beat procrastination?
- ✔ What methods should I use? Flash cards? Re-reading my notes? Highlighting?

Luckily, you no longer need to guess at the answers. Education researchers have looked at all the available revision studies, and the jury is in. They've come up with some key pointers on the best ways to revise, as well as some thoughts on popular revision methods that aren't so helpful. The next few pages will help you understand what we know about the best revision methods.

How can I beat procrastination?

This is an age-old question, and it applies to adults as well! Have a look at our top three tips below.

Reward yourself

When we think a task we have to do is going to be boring, hard or uncomfortable, we often put if off and do something more 'fun' instead. But we often don't really enjoy the 'fun' activity because we feel guilty about avoiding what we should be doing. Instead, get your work done and promise yourself a reward after you complete it. Whatever treat you choose will seem all the sweeter, and you'll feel proud for doing something you found difficult. Just do it!

Just do it!

We tend to procrastinate when we think the task we have to do is going to be difficult or dull. The funny thing is, the most uncomfortable part is usually making ourselves sit down and start it in the first place. Once you begin, it's usually not nearly as bad as you anticipated.

Pomodoro technique

The pomodoro technique helps you trick your brain by telling it you only have to focus for a short time. Set a timer for 20 minutes and focus that whole period on your revision. Turn off your phone, clear your desk, and work. At the end of the 20 minutes, you get to take a break for five. Then, do another 20 minutes. You'll usually find your rhythm and it becomes easier to carry on because it's only for a short, defined chunk of time.

Spaced practice

We tend to arrange our revision into big blocks. For example, you might tell yourself: "This week I'll do all my revision for the Cold War, then next week I'll do the Medicine Through Time unit."

REVISION SUGGESTIONS

This is called **massed practice**, because all revision for a single topic is done as one big mass.

But there's a better way! Try **spaced practice** instead. Instead of putting all revision sessions for one topic into a single block, space them out. See the example below for how it works.

This means planning ahead, rather than leaving revision to the last minute - but the evidence strongly suggests it's worth it. You'll remember much more from your revision if you use **spaced practice** rather than organising it into big blocks. Whichever method you choose, though, remember to reward yourself with breaks.

Spaced practice (more effective):

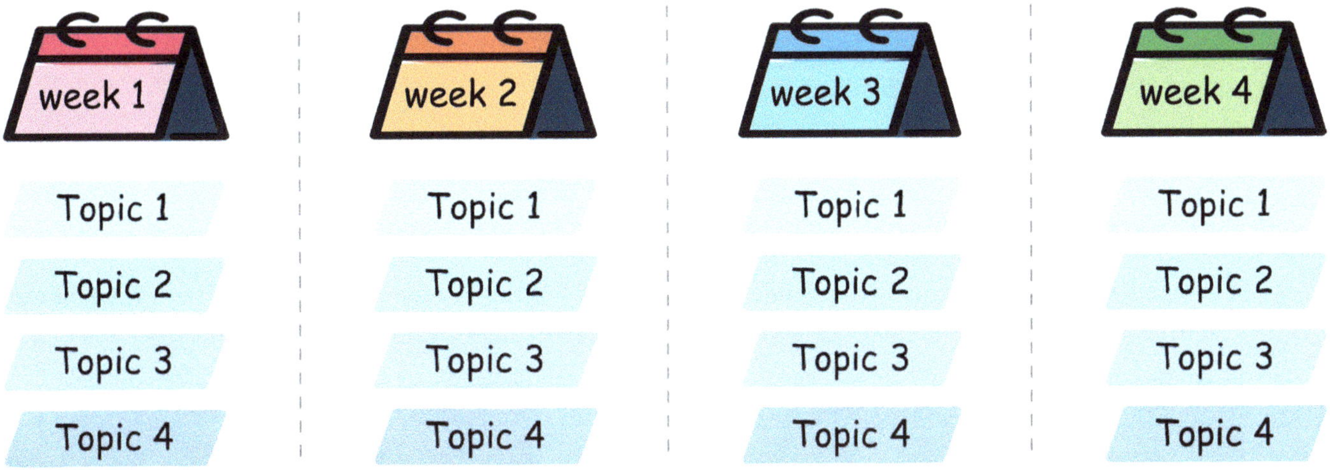

week 1	week 2	week 3	week 4
Topic 1	Topic 1	Topic 1	Topic 1
Topic 2	Topic 2	Topic 2	Topic 2
Topic 3	Topic 3	Topic 3	Topic 3
Topic 4	Topic 4	Topic 4	Topic 4

Massed practice (less effective)

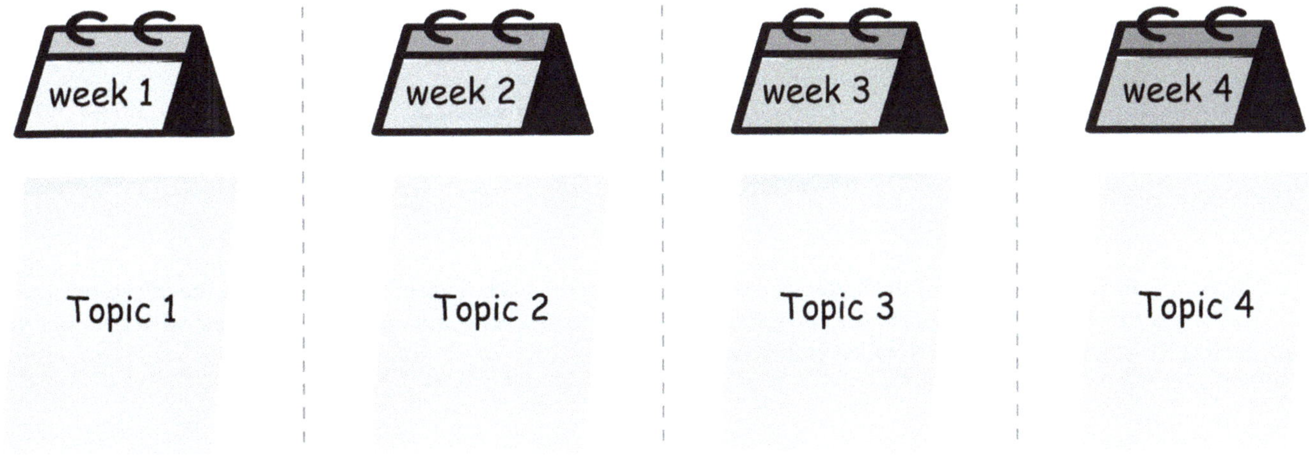

week 1	week 2	week 3	week 4
Topic 1	Topic 2	Topic 3	Topic 4

Get our free app at GCSEHistory.com

REVISION SUGGESTIONS

What methods should I use to revise?

Self-testing/flash cards **Self explanation/mind-mapping**

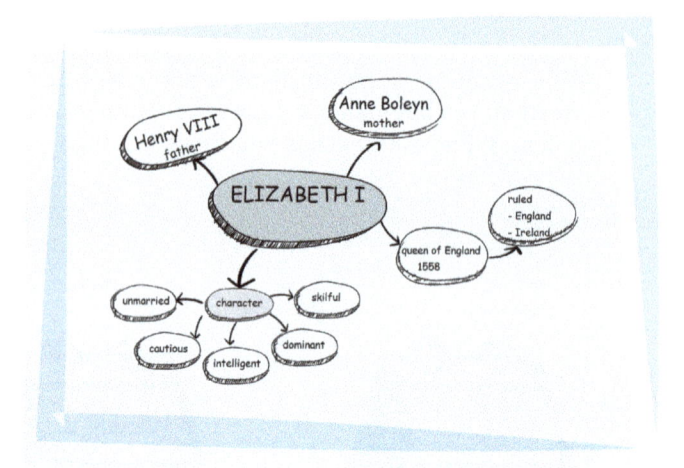

The research shows a clear winner for revision methods - **self-testing**. A good way to do this is with **flash cards**. Flash cards are really useful for helping you recall short – but important – pieces of information, like names and dates.

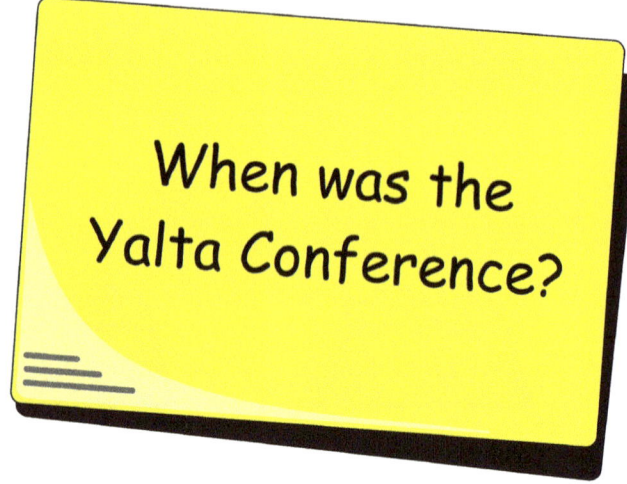

Side A - question

Side B - answer

Write questions on one side of the cards, and the answers on the back. This makes answering the questions and then testing yourself easy. Put all the cards you get right in a pile to one side, and only repeat the test with the ones you got wrong - this will force you to work on your weaker areas.

pile with right answers

pile with wrong answers

As this book has a quiz question structure itself, you can use it for this technique.

Another good revision method is **self-explanation**. This is where you explain how and why one piece of information from your course linked with another piece.

This can be done with **mind-maps**, where you draw the links and then write explanations for how they connect. For example, President Truman is connected with anti-communism because of the Truman Doctrine.

Quizzes, amazing exam preparation tools and more at GCSEHistory.com

REVISION SUGGESTIONS

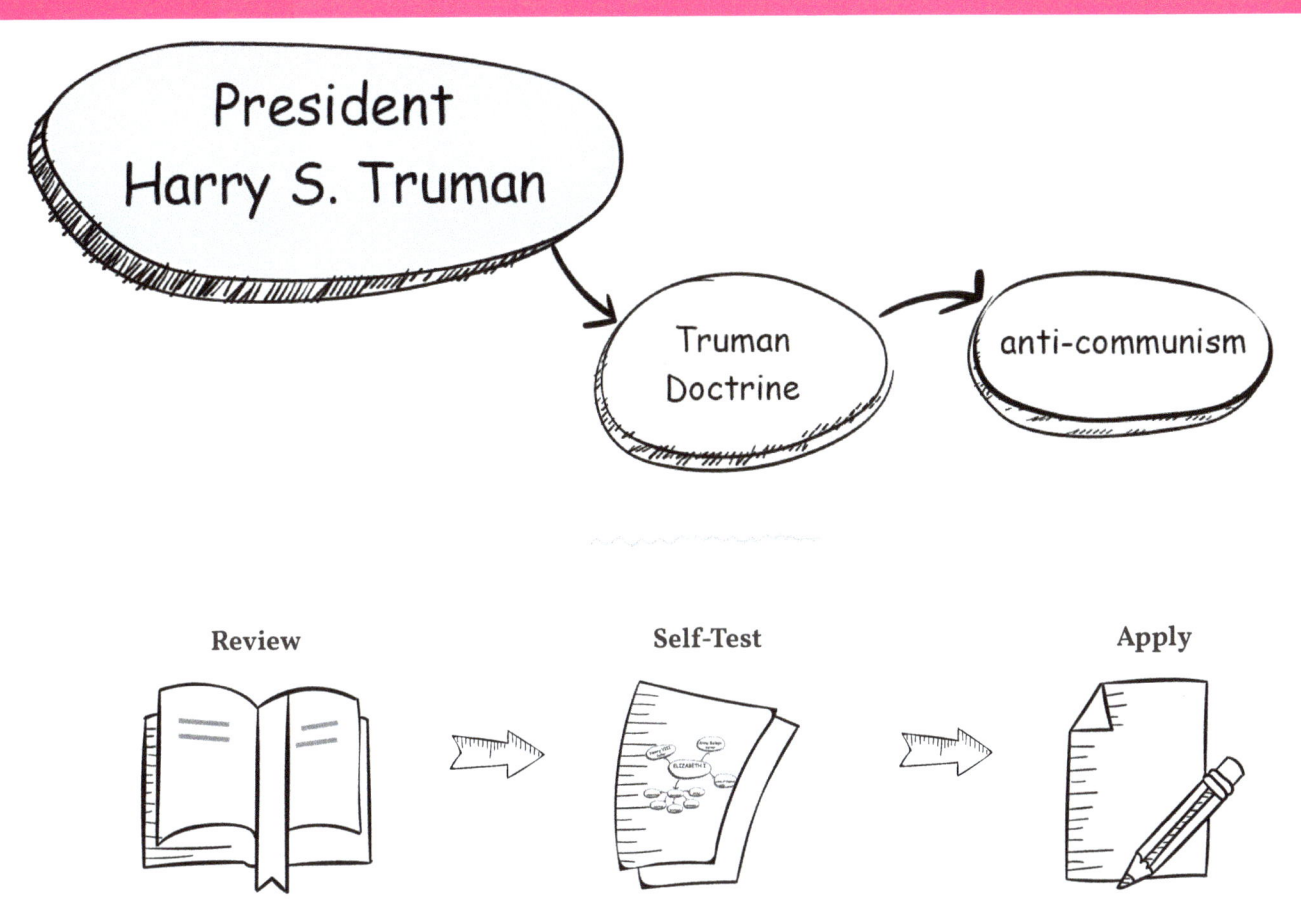

President Harry S. Truman → Truman Doctrine → anti-communism

Review

Start by highlighting or re-reading to create your flashcards for self-testing.

Self-Test

Test yourself with flash cards. Make mind maps to explain the concepts.

Apply

Apply your knowledge on practice exam questions.

Which revision techniques should I be cautious about?

Highlighting and **re-reading** are not necessarily bad strategies - but the research does say they're less effective than flash cards and mind-maps.

Highlighting

Re-reading

If you do use these methods, make sure they are **the first step to creating flash cards**. Really engage with the material as you go, rather than switching to autopilot.

Get our free app at GCSEHistory.com

CHINA: CONFLICT, CRISIS AND CHANGE, 1900-89

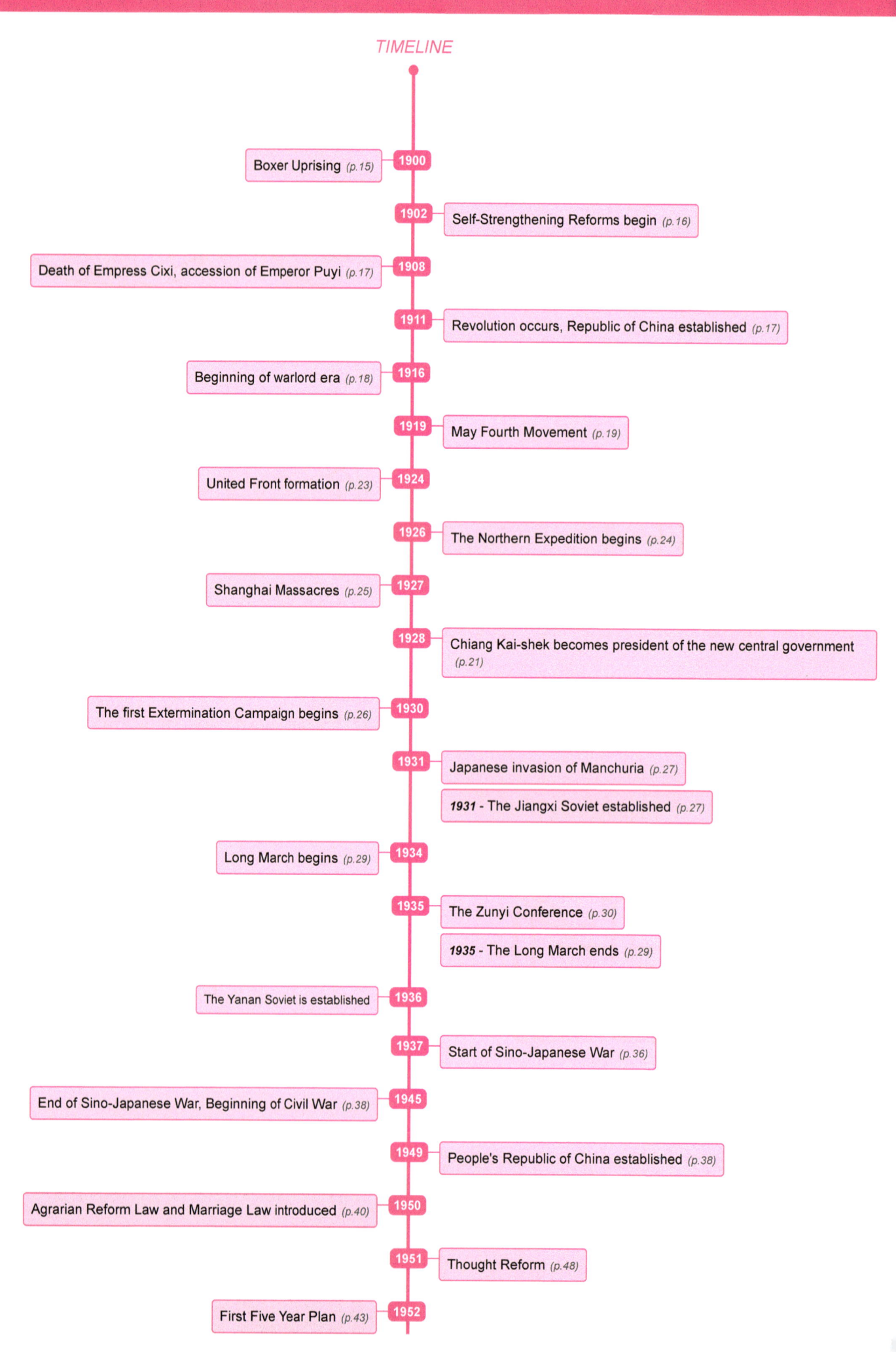

TIMELINE

- **1900** — Boxer Uprising *(p.15)*
- **1902** — Self-Strengthening Reforms begin *(p.16)*
- **1908** — Death of Empress Cixi, accession of Emperor Puyi *(p.17)*
- **1911** — Revolution occurs, Republic of China established *(p.17)*
- **1916** — Beginning of warlord era *(p.18)*
- **1919** — May Fourth Movement *(p.19)*
- **1924** — United Front formation *(p.23)*
- **1926** — The Northern Expedition begins *(p.24)*
- **1927** — Shanghai Massacres *(p.25)*
- **1928** — Chiang Kai-shek becomes president of the new central government *(p.21)*
- **1930** — The first Extermination Campaign begins *(p.26)*
- **1931** — Japanese invasion of Manchuria *(p.27)*
- **1931** — The Jiangxi Soviet established *(p.27)*
- **1934** — Long March begins *(p.29)*
- **1935** — The Zunyi Conference *(p.30)*
- **1935** — The Long March ends *(p.29)*
- **1936** — The Yanan Soviet is established
- **1937** — Start of Sino-Japanese War *(p.36)*
- **1945** — End of Sino-Japanese War, Beginning of Civil War *(p.38)*
- **1949** — People's Republic of China established *(p.38)*
- **1950** — Agrarian Reform Law and Marriage Law introduced *(p.40)*
- **1951** — Thought Reform *(p.48)*
- **1952** — First Five Year Plan *(p.43)*

CHINA: CONFLICT, CRISIS AND CHANGE, 1900-89

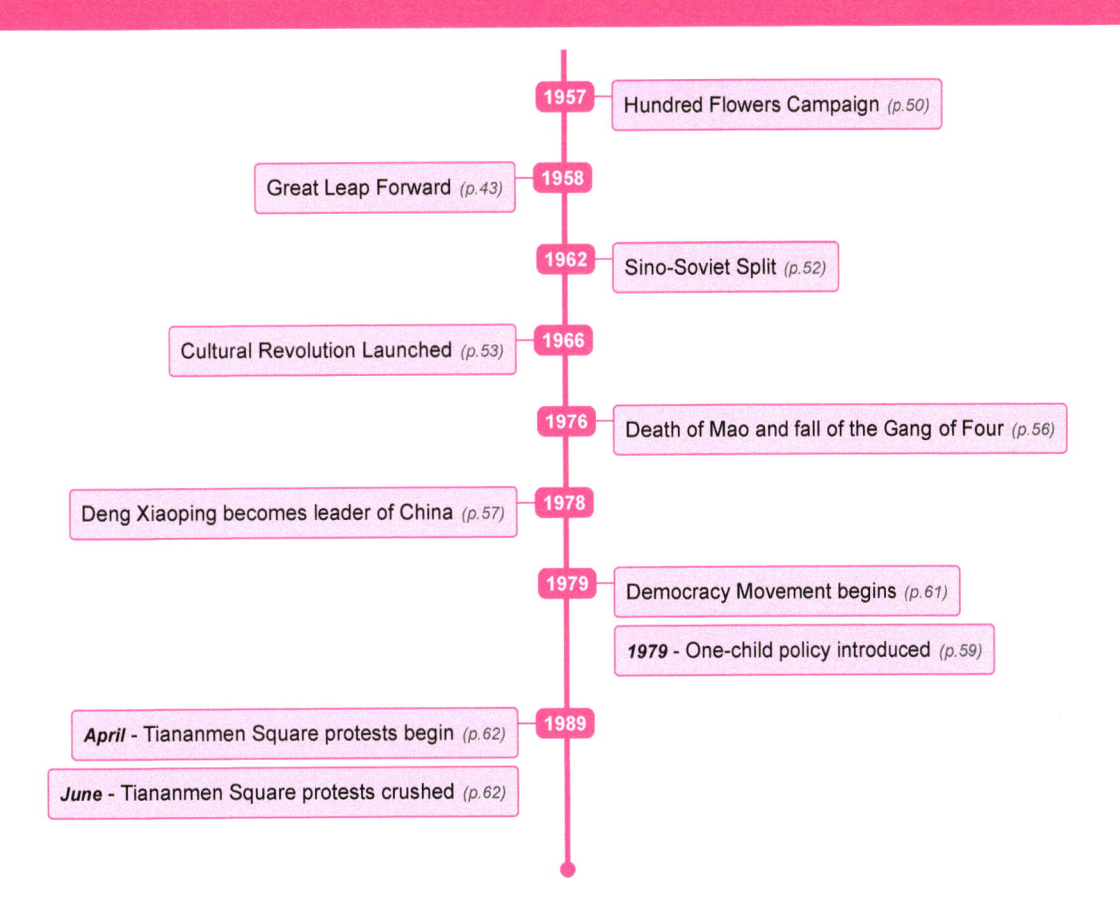

- **1957** — Hundred Flowers Campaign *(p.50)*
- **1958** — Great Leap Forward *(p.43)*
- **1962** — Sino-Soviet Split *(p.52)*
- **1966** — Cultural Revolution Launched *(p.53)*
- **1976** — Death of Mao and fall of the Gang of Four *(p.56)*
- **1978** — Deng Xiaoping becomes leader of China *(p.57)*
- **1979** — Democracy Movement begins *(p.61)*
- *1979* - One-child policy introduced *(p.59)*
- **1989**
  - *April* - Tiananmen Square protests begin *(p.62)*
  - *June* - Tiananmen Square protests crushed *(p.62)*

CHINA IN 1900

In the mid-19th century, China was one of the most powerful countries in the world. However, by the turn of the 20th century, foreign powers were threatening to dominate it.

What was the position of China in 1900?
China was a powerful country in 1900. It was the largest country in Asia, had vast natural resources and was a strong producer of goods.

Who ruled China in 1900?
In 1900, China's 300 million population was ruled by Zaitian. He was the 11th and penultimate emperor of the Qing dynasty.

Where did China control in 1900?
China's borders stretched from Manchuria in the north east, down to the borders of Burma and Laos in the south, and across to Tibet and Xinjiang in the west.

Why was China in decline in early the 1900s?
In 1900, China began to see a decline for 3 reasons:

- ✓ China had been defeated in the Opium Wars between 1839 and 1860. It was feeling the consequences, which included Britain taking valuable resources from China.
- ✓ China had also been defeated in the 1894 war with Japan, which resulted in it losing control of Korea.
- ✓ France had also gained territory in the south of the Chinese empire. They gained Vietnam during the Sino-French War of 1884-85.

DID YOU KNOW?

China had the largest population on earth in 1900!

China was home to nearly 25% of the world's population, with 400,000,000 million people living there. This was more than in the whole of the British Empire.

RULING IN THE COUNTRY

'I have often thought that I am the most clever woman that ever lived and others cannot compare with me…although I have heard much about Queen Victoria.' Dowager Empress Cixi, 1800s

What was the system of ruling in China?
China was ruled by an imperial system with one person having complete control over the empire.

Who ruled China?
China was ruled by an emperor. This wasn't limited to one family but worked on the basis that any dynasty could rule so long as fate favoured them.

When was China ruled by emperors?

China was ruled by various emperors and dynasties from 1570 BC to AD 1912.

Why was China ruled by emperors?

People believed in the 'Mandate of Heaven'. This suggested that fate had chosen the emperor, and this should be respected as part of the world's natural order.

> **DID YOU KNOW?**
>
> **The system of dynasties ruling in China had existed for centuries!**
> One of China's first emperors (Qin Shi Huang, 259 BC –210 BC) was buried with over 8,000 terracotta soldiers to protect him in the afterlife. This is a famous tourist attraction and can still be visited today.

THE BOXER UPRISING

With decreasing influence, European powers began to cement their positions within China. The Boxer Uprising was sparked by resentment at this change in power but would end in even more concessions being granted to foreign nations.

What was the Boxer Uprising?

The Boxer Uprising was an anti-foreigner attack led by Chinese peasants.

Who led the Boxer Uprising?

A secret organisation, the Society of Righteous and Harmonious Fists, began the attacks before they became more widespread among peasants.

When did the Boxer Uprising happen?

The Boxer Uprising took place between 2nd November 1899 and 7th September 1901.

Why did the Boxer Uprising happen?

There were 3 main causes of the Boxer Uprising:

- During an attempt to modernise, Emperor Guangxu was overthrown by his aunt, Empress Dowager Cixi. Cixi opposed the privileges being given to foreigners in China.
- The Chinese had a deep-rooted hatred towards the 'foreign devils', as they were seen to be changing the usual way of life and attacking the traditional religions.
- As a way of avoiding criticism, Cixi promoted the 'foreign devils' as a common enemy of the people. She scapegoated them and encouraged violent attacks against them.

What were the key events of the Boxer Uprising?

There were 7 key events which happened during the Boxer Uprising:

- Peasants had suffered from many natural disasters during the late 1890s.
- The Boxers began attacking foreigners and Christians.

- ☑ Attacks started in the east coast province of Shandong before spreading further north east to locations such as Shanxi.
- ☑ The uprising arrived in Beijing and the German ambassador, Clemens von Ketteler, was killed.
- ☑ Panicked, westerners sought refuge in the British Legation. Around 3,000 westerners and Chinese Christians were besieged for 55 days.
- ☑ Cixi backed the Boxers and declared war. However, the forces were unable to overcome the legation's defences. An international military force was sent, which defeated the Boxers.
- ☑ Cixi, escaping potential capture, hid herself as a peasant among the population and fled to Xian.

What was the impact of the Boxer Uprising?

There were 5 key consequences for the failed Boxer Uprising, which continued to weaken China:

- ☑ The Qing dynasty suffered damage to its reputation. This imposed another Western defeat on the Chinese.
- ☑ The Chinese were forced to pay reparations of $330 million over the next 39 years.
- ☑ China's military fortifications, defences and weapons were destroyed.
- ☑ International forces were permanently placed in locations across Beijing and 10 officials were executed for their roles.
- ☑ The failed attempt to get rid of foreigners convinced Cixi that reforms must happen. However, the reforms were unsuccessful and led to the fall of the Qing dynasty in 1911.

DID YOU KNOW?

Some of the reparations from the Boxer Uprising were spent in China!

Tsinghua University in Beijing was opened on 11th April, 1911 using reparations funds issued under the Boxer Protocol.

SELF-STRENGTHENING REFORM, 1902-11

'Learn barbarian (Western) methods to combat barbarian threats.'
Wei Yuan, 1843

What were the self-strengthening reforms?

These were a series of education, monetary, military, political and commercial reforms. They aimed at modernising China through learning and copying Western methods, and technology from the countries with a presence in China.

Who introduced the self-strengthening reforms?

The reforms were introduced by Empress Dowager Cixi.

When were the self-strengthening reforms introduced?

The reforms were introduced over a number of years, between 1902 and 1911.

Why were the self-strengthening reforms introduced?

Cixi introduced the reforms for 3 main reasons:

- ☑ She needed to secure her dynasty following the embarrassment and consequences of the Boxer Uprising (p. 15).
- ☑ As foreigners were even stronger in China, Cixi decided to use their knowledge to help her advance her country.

- Little progress had been made in the late 1800s and Cixi needed to take quick action to improve her dynasty's reputation.

What changes did the self-strengthening reforms introduce?

There were 7 key changes which occurred during the reforms:

- 1902: Foot binding was banned.
- 1905: Traditional examinations for civil service positions were removed in an attempt to improve diversity in the sector, which was traditionally heavily Mandarin.
- 1908: A new army was established.
- 1909: Provisional assemblies were introduced.
- 1910-11: National Consultative Council established to help advise the government.
- Educational reforms were introduced, with more opportunities for military service and international scholarships.
- The railways were nationalised to offer more consistency and control in transportation.

> **DID YOU KNOW?**
>
> **Foot-binding was performed to intentionally make women's feet smaller.**
>
> Small feet were considered more attractive to men and, therefore, important for potential marriages. It was a painful process for young girls, involving the toes being bound beneath the foot.

THE 1911 REVOLUTION

'For 50 years Cixi's was the brain, hers the strong hand that held in check the rising forces of disintegration; and when she died it required no great gifts of divination to foretell the approaching doom.'
John Bland, 1910

What was the 1911 revolution in China?

The 1911 revolution saw the removal of the Qing dynasty and the creation of the Republic of China.

What caused the 1911 revolution in China?

There were 6 key causes of the 1911 revolution:

- After the death of Emperor Guangxu and Empress Cixi in November 1908, Emperor Puyi took the throne. He was just 2 years old, which left an inexperienced Prince Chun leading a weak government.
- The self-strengthening reforms had little impact and people wanted quicker reform.
- Due to the cost of some reforms, taxes had to be increased. This made the dynasty unpopular.
- Prince Chun sacked General Yuan Shikai as he believed he was becoming too powerful. This created a strong enemy and who could be an alternative leader to the Qing dynasty.
- The exiled Sun Yat-sen *(p.20)* was promoting ideas of nationalism and republicanism for China. These had become popular with those studying abroad under the reforms.
- The nationalisation of the railways had proved controversial. Owners were not compensated.

What were the key events of the 1911 revolution in China?

There were 5 key events in the 1911 revolution:

- 9th October 1911: An accidental explosion caused by revolutionaries in Hankou made people think a revolution had started. This led to outbreaks of discontent across the city and country.
- 10th October 1911: Wuhan soldiers started a mutiny which spread rapidly across China. It became known as the 'Double Tenth' uprising.
- Within 6 weeks, all except 3 provinces had declared their independence.
- 1st November 1911: The Qing dynasty recalled General Yuan Shikai as prime minister and charged him with putting down the rebellion. This failed, as he later switched sides to support the revolution.
- On 1st January 1912, Sun Yat-sen (p.20) returned from exile to briefly become president of the new Republic of China.

What was the impact of the 1911 revolution in China?

There were 5 consequences arising from the 1911 revolution:

- The revolution ended 2,200 years of imperial rule in China.
- Sun Yat-sen (p.20) stepped down, with General Yuan Shikai replacing him as president, in return for the removal of the imperial system.
- General Yuan Shikai forced the abdication of Emperor Puyi on 12th February, 1912.
- The power vacuum allowed General Yuan Shikai to become the dictator of China, including an attempt to make himself emperor in 1915.
- The army revolted against General Yuan Shikai due to his acceptance of Japan's demands for influence in China. Shortly after, in June 1916 he died of a stroke, which left China without a designated leader.

DID YOU KNOW?

Emperor Guangxu's death is still a mystery!
100 years after his death, it was confirmed Emperor Guangxu had high levels of arsenic in his system. This suggested he was poisoned. Empress Cixi has been suggested as a suspect, but the truth remains unknown.

THE ERA OF THE WARLORDS, 1916-27

Following the end of dynastic rule, a power vacuum emerged and China found itself divided into provinces ruled by individual warlords. As the warlords strove to increase their power, battles erupted and China further weakened itself against foreign influence.

What was the warlords era in China?

This was a period of time after General Yuan Shikai's death, where individual generals ruled their own local provinces.

When was the warlords era in China?

The warlords era in China lasted from the death of General Yuan Shikai in 1916 to 1927.

Who were the warlords in China?

Warlords were usually local generals who seized control of their provinces. There were hundreds of these generals, who each ruled their province differently.

Who were the most powerful warlords in China?

3 of the more powerful warlords were:

- ✓ Feng Yuxiang ruled with a Christian mentality and believed in ruling his province morally.
- ✓ However, Zhang Zongchang was a violent ruler who ruled with fear against any opposition.
- ✓ Similarly, Zhang Zuolin used extreme violence and punishments against his own men to warn them against rebellion.

Why did the warlords era in China happen?

There was a power vacuum after General Yuan Shikai's death, and no one could secure the power to rule with the same authority. However, the local generals appointed by Yuan Shikai had enough power to rule their own provinces.

What were the consequences of the warlords era in China?

Due to the harsh treatment meted out by the majority of the warlords, and ineffective individual responses from the provinces to natural disasters, many people began turning to more radical ideas.

DID YOU KNOW?

Even a trip to the theatre could cost you your life in warlord-era China!

Zhang Zuolin beheaded two soldiers for failing to pay for their tickets at the local theatre.

THE MAY FOURTH MOVEMENT, 1919

'A constitutional republic which does not derive from the conscious realisation and voluntary action of the majority of the people is a bogus republic and bogus constitutionalism.'
Chen Duxiu, 1916

What was the May Fourth movement?

The May Fourth movement was a protest against the Treaty of Versailles, and in particular the land reparations term which could see Chinese territories given to Japan.

Who led the May Fourth movement?

Students from Beijing University formed the majority of protesters, including a young Mao Zedong *(p.31)*. This later spread to other cities and workers.

When was the May Fourth movement?

The movement was formed during the Treaty of Versailles negotiations. Formal protests began on 4th May, 1919.

What were the demands of the May Fourth movement?

The movement demanded that the principle of national self-determination be applied to China.

What were the consequences of the May Fourth movement?

There were 4 consequences of the May Fourth movement:

- ✓ The Chinese refused to sign the Treaty of Versailles.
- ✓ This movement generated a rejection of traditional principles in China. These ranged from the way in which China was governed to marriage practices.

- ☑ There was a growth of 'new ideas' such as democracy and equal rights in China, which became known as the 'new tide'.
- ☑ The 'new tide' demanded the unity of China under one democratic government and the removal of Western privileges in China.

> **DID YOU KNOW?**
>
> **Many see the May Fourth Movement as the birth of the Communist Party in China.**
>
> Many leading figures in the movement, such as Chen Duxiu and Li Dazhao, would go on to found the Chinese Communist Party.

SUN YAT-SEN

'A republic has been established, and our compatriots in Mongolia, Tibet, Qinghai and Xinjiang, who have always been a part of China, are all now Chinese citizens who are masters of their country.'
Sun Yat-sen, 1912

Who was Sun Yat-sen?

Dr Sun Yat-sen was a Chinese nationalist revolutionary who formed the Guomindang (p.22) (GMD) in 1919.

What was Sun Yat-sen's background?

There were 4 key events in Sun Yat-sen's life:

- ☑ Born in Guangdong, Sun Yat-sen moved to Hawaii with his older brother.
- ☑ He was educated in Hawaii and learned English before moving to Hong Kong and converting to Christianity.
- ☑ He held strong nationalist beliefs and attempted a rebellion in Guangzhou during 1895. This failed and he went into exile, travelling across Europe.
- ☑ He returned to China in 1911 to become president, before handing control to the more powerful General Yuan. When the general died, Sun Yat-sen returned to China in 1917.

What were the key events of Sun Yat-sen's return to China?

There were 4 key events when Sun Yat-sen returned to China in 1917:

- ☑ In 1919, he set up a nationalistic government party called the Guomindang (p.22) (GMD).
- ☑ He formulated the 'Three Principles of the People', which outlined the GMD's policy. This was to remove foreign control from China, to allow for democracy in China, and to solve poverty by developing state ownership of industries.
- ☑ In 1924, he formed the National Revolutionary Army (NRA) to help fight and overthrow the warlords.
- ☑ He also worked with the Bolshevik government to secure weapons for the war against the warlords.

When did Sun Yat-sen live?

Sun Yat-sen was born in 1866 and died of cancer in 1925.

> **DID YOU KNOW?**
>
> **When in exile, Sun Yat-sen was kidnapped!**
>
> He stayed in London while in exile. Every Sunday he would walk to the British Museum, and one day he was bundled into a Chinese diplomatic house. However, following public pressure and media attention, Sun Yat-sen was released without harm.

CHIANG KAI-SHEK

'War is not only a matter of equipment, artillery, group troops or air force; it is largely a matter of spirit, or morale.'
Chiang Kai-shek

Who was Chiang Kai-shek?

Chiang Kai-shek was a Chinese nationalist, politician and general. He led the Guomindang *(p.22)* (GMD), often referred to as the Chinese Nationalist Party, and was leader of the Republic of China until his defeat in the Chinese Civil War *(p.38)*.

When did Chiang Kai-shek live?

Chiang was born in 1887 and died in 1975. He ruled mainland China from 1928 until 1949, and Taiwan from 1949 until his death.

Where was Chiang Kai-shek born?

Chiang was born in Xikou, China.

What was Chiang Kai-shek's role?

Chiang played 3 key roles during his life:

- He was one of the founding figures of the Chinese Nationalist Party *(p.22)* (GMD).
- By the mid 1920s, he had consolidated power and became ruler of the Republic of China in 1928.
- He waged war on the CCP *(p.22)* and Japan, before being defeated by the CCP in 1949. He fled China for Taiwan where he was president until his death in 1975.

> **DID YOU KNOW?**
>
> **One man with two names....Chiang Kai-shek is also Jiang Jieshi!**
>
> The spelling used in this study guide is based upon the Giles-Wade system of spelling, which was created in 19th century based on the pronunciation of words. However, the modern system (pin-yin) calls him Jiang Jieshi.

Get our free app at GCSEHistory.com

GUOMINDANG

The Guomindang was formed in the build up to the 1911 Revolution as the 'Revolutionary Army'. Its constant battles with the communists would eventually see its downfall in mainland China.

What was the Guomindang?
The Guomindang (also referred to as the GMD or Kuomintang / KMT), was a nationalistic political party which operated in China from 1919-49.

What were the Guomindang beliefs?
The Guomindang had 3 key beliefs:
- They believed in the 'Three Principles of the People' - nationalism, democracy, and economic reform.
- This included the establishment of a republic to rule China.
- The Guomindang also promoted common political features to that of European fascism, e.g. one central leader.

Why was the Guomindang formed?
The Guomindang was formed to create a united nationalist front, which would seize power from the various warlords and unite China to create a single state.

When was the Guomindang formed?
The GMD was founded in October 1919, though early forms and members of the group are seen in the Revolutionary Alliance (1905) and the Nationalist Party (1912).

Who founded the Guomindang?
The group was founded by Sun Yat-sen *(p.20)* and Liao Chongzhen. Sun Yat-sen would become the group's first president.

DID YOU KNOW?

The Guomindang still exists today...in Taiwan.

The party ruled over Taiwan (or officially the Republic of China) from 1928 to 2000. It is now one of the opposition parties in Taiwan's government.

THE EMERGENCE OF THE CHINESE COMMUNIST PARTY

Formed as a challenge to the Guomindang in 1921, the Chinese Communist Party would struggle to survive in its early years. However, it would win the long battle to control China.

What was the Chinese Communist Party?
The Chinese Communist Party (CCP) was a group which wanted to bring a communist system to China.

What were the Chinese Communist Party beliefs?
The Chinese Communist Party had 4 central beliefs:
- A system in which all people would be equal across China.
- State control of the economy.

- ✓ Redistribution of wealth.
- ✓ Dictatorship of the proletariat.

Why was the Chinese Communist Party formed?

China was similar to Russia in terms of politics and economy. It was believed China could mirror and recreate a similar revolution to the Russian Revolution of 1917.

When was the Chinese Communist Party formed?

It was founded in June 1921.

Who founded the Chinese Communist Party?

Chen Duxiu became the group's first general secretary, with Mao Zedong *(p.31)* appointed to the leadership.

Who influenced the Chinese Communist Party?

Bolshevik influencers suggested the CCP join forces with the GMD, as they were both ideologically similar and the CCP was too small to lead a revolution alone. As the CCP was funded by the Bolsheviks, the leadership agreed and merged as a sub-group of the GMD.

DID YOU KNOW?

Big trees grow from little acorns!

This was certainly the case for the CCP, which had only 50 members to begin with in 1921.

THE ESTABLISHMENT OF THE UNITED FRONT

The Guomindang and the Chinese Communist Party joined forces in order to establish singular command over warlord-controlled China. However, this uneasy alliance would not last long.

What was the First United Front?

The First United Front was a coalition between the GMD and CCP *(p.22)* during the warlord era *(p.18)* in China.

What were the First United Front aims?

The First United Front had 3 main aims:

- ✓ The removal and destruction of warlord control in China.
- ✓ The expulsion of foreign interests and control in China.
- ✓ To improve everyday life for the Chinese population.

When did the First United Front operate?

The First United Front was formed in 1924 and lasted until April 1927.

Why did the First United Front end?

The First United Front ended early (before the completion of its aims) due to the Shanghai Massacres. This was where communists were arrested, attacked and killed on the orders of Chiang Kai-shek *(p.21)*. This formalised the split between the GMD and CCP *(p.22)*.

DID YOU KNOW?

Things were pretty one-sided.

The CCP only referred to the relationship as the United Front. The GMD saw the collaboration differently, referring to it as the 'admission of the communists' to the party.

THE NORTHERN EXPEDITION

The United Front's campaign was successful. However, at Shanghai during the Northern Expedition, tensions would flare and see the CCP and GMD come to blows.

What was the Northern Expedition?

The Northern Expedition was an attack on the warlords and the areas they controlled.

What was the Northern Expedition's aim?

The expedition force was to surround and starve each warlord army in order to defeat it, while gaining support from the peasants by offering food.

Who led the Northern Expedition?

The Northern Expedition was led by the leader of the GMD, Chiang Kai-shek *(p.21)*. It used the GMD's highly effective National Revolutionary Army (NRA).

When was the Northern Expedition?

The Northern Expedition ran from 9th July, 1926, until 29th December, 1928.

Why was the Northern Expedition launched?

The expedition was sparked following an incident in May 1925. A British commander shot and killed 12 Chinese people in Shanghai. This inspired the United Front to take immediate action against the warlords who allowed such foreign influence.

What was the Northern Expedition's outcome?

The United Front was victorious in this strategy. By April 1928, all warlords had been defeated, with the GMD declaring a national government. However, tensions had emerged between the GMD and the CCP *(p.22)*, which led to CCP withdrawing from the United Front in April 1927.

What were the reasons for the success of the Northern Expedition?

There were 3 reasons for the success of the United Front:

- ✓ The forces of the United Front heavily outnumbered the individual warlord armies.

- The communists helped gain the support of local peasants.
- Negotiations with some warlords meant the GMD was able to take control of the provinces peacefully, in return for warlords being able to keep their own private armies.

> **DID YOU KNOW?**
>
> **Britain tried to negotiate and protect its interests in China.**
>
> Britain issued the December Memorandum to assure the Nationalists, but this was seen as lip service. Britain even tried to get Japan involved in joint action, but the Japanese were unwilling to get involved in a conflict which was of little interest to them.

THE SHANGHAI MASSACRES

The GMD's purge of the CCP marked the end of the alliance and the beginning of the 'white terror', which would force many communists into hiding. Many marked this as the beginning of the Chinese Civil War.

What were the Shanghai Massacres?
The Shanghai Massacres were part of a campaign of planned attacks and murders of communists in Shanghai.

Who led the Shanghai Massacres?
The GMD led the attacks and were supported by other groups such as the Green Gang. Together, they murdered over 5,000 communists.

When did the Shanghai Massacres happen?
The Shanghai Massacres took place on 12th April, 1927. However, attacks in other areas continued for weeks after.

Why did the Shanghai Massacres happen?
The GMD attacked the communists in order to gain the loyalty of the industrialists and foreigners, who were worried about losing their interests in the area should the communists take control.

Where did the Shanghai Massacres happen?
The Shanghai Massacres started in Shanghai, before spreading to other provinces such as Hunan.

What was the impact of the Shanghai Massacres?
Along with the deaths of 5,000 communists, this also brought an end to the First United Front *(p.23)*. It would also lead to the GMD Extermination Campaigns.

> **DID YOU KNOW?**
>
> **You didn't want to get on Du Yuesheng's bad side.**
>
> The leader of the 'Green Gang' which helped commit the Shanghai Massacres was a mastermind criminal and drug lord. By 1927, Du Yuesheng had made over $50 million in profit from his underworld organisation.

Get our free app at GCSEHistory.com

THE EXTERMINATION CAMPAIGNS

With the CCP on the back foot, the GMD looked to force home its advantage with a series of military campaigns against the CCP. While not hugely successful, the GMD did eventually force the CCP to flee.

What were the Extermination Campaigns?
The Extermination Campaigns were a series of attacks on the communists to try and destroy them completely.

When were the Extermination Campaigns?
They took place between October 1930 and October 1934.

Who led the Extermination Campaigns?
The campaigns were led by Chiang Kai-shek *(p.21)* and the National Revolutionary Army (NRA).

What were the main Extermination Campaigns?
There were 4 key events:
- October 1930: 44,000 NRA troops attacked communists in Jiangxi. The attack failed due to the communists using guerrilla warfare tactics.
- July 1931: 100,000 NRA troops attacked the communists, but the nationalist soldiers' caution allowed the communists to escape.
- Autumn 1933: The final campaign was launched. Using a scorched earth policy, the GMD forced the communists to fight. By October, the communists were heavily defeated and forced to retreat.
- A number of other campaigns took place, but these often failed due to lack of support from the peasants. They viewed the GMD as violent aggressors, and were themselves victims of brutality by Chiang's men.

What were the results of the Extermination Campaigns?
There were 4 main outcomes from the Extermination Campaigns:
- Over 500,000 peasants were killed by the GMD.
- The communists lost over 60,000 soldiers.
- The communists lost control of the Jiangxi Soviet *(p.27)* and were forced to flee, which forced them to seek a new base area.
- Some would argue this was the first battle of the civil war between the GMD and CCP *(p.22)*, following the Shanghai Massacres.

DID YOU KNOW?

There was significant influence from Germany!

The GMD had German advisers, Hans von Seeckt and Alexander von Falkenhausen, to help devise and launch a plan. When Adolf Hitler came to power the cooperation continued, as the GMD and the Nazis shared similar ideologies.

MANCHURIA, 1931

'I do not think there is the slightest prospect of any war.'
Viscount Cecil in 1931 to the League of Nations, one week before the invasion

What was the Mukden incident?
The Japanese had ambitions to take over Manchuria, and used the Mukden incident as an excuse to launch an invasion.

Why did the Mukden incident happen?
Japan wanted to expand its borders into Manchuria but needed a reason to do so; the Mukden incident proved perfect.

Where did the Mukden incident happen?
The Mukden incident happened on the South Manchurian railway.

What were the key events in the Mukden incident?
There were 5 key events:
- On 18th September, 1931, there was an explosion on a Japanese-owned railway in South Manchuria.
- The Japanese blamed the Chinese, saying the train had been attacked by Chinese soldiers. However, the Japanese had set off the explosion themselves.
- The Chinese government denied any involvement, stating all its soldiers were asleep at the time.
- In 'retaliation', the Kwantung army invaded Manchuria.
- Japan renamed Manchuria as Manchukuo, and put former Chinese emperor Pu Yi in charge. He was a puppet ruler, controlled by the Japanese army.

Who was involved in the Mukden incident?
The Kwantung, or Japanese army, were behind the Mukden incident.

What were the results of the Mukden incident?
This Mukden incident resulted in Japan invading Manchuria and triggering an international crisis.

DID YOU KNOW?

The failure to solve the Manchurian crisis is one factor which led to the eventual downfall of the League of Nations.

The League demanded Japan leave Manchuria. However, it refused and left the League of Nations. This caused great embarrassment and showed how weak the League was.

THE JIANGXI SOVIET

Established in 1931, this was the CCP stronghold during the Extermination Campaigns. It would offer good protection until October 1934, when the CCP was forced to flee to avoid destruction.

What was the Jiangxi Soviet?
The Jiangxi Soviet was a communist state set up by Mao Zedong *(p.31)* during the Chinese Civil War *(p.38)*.

Who was involved in the Jiangxi Soviet?

The CCP *(p.22)*, under the leadership of Mao Zedong *(p.31)*, ruled the Jiangxi Soviet. There were over 3 million citizens defended by 130,000 Red Army troops.

When did the Jiangxi Soviet exist?

The Jiangxi Soviet was founded in November 1931 and destroyed in October 1934.

Where did the Jiangxi Soviet happen?

The Jiangxi Soviet was located in the province of Jiangxi in eastern China.

What happened at the Jiangxi Soviet?

There were 9 key events during the Jiangxi Soviet period:

- Mao Zedong *(p.31)* and Zhu De set up the Chinese Soviet Republic. This was its own country with Mao as CCP *(p.22)* party secretary and Zhu as head of the Red Army.
- Mao introduced a Land Law in 1930 that redistributed land to the majority of peasants in the Soviet.
- The communists reduced taxes, reduced corruption, set up schools and hospitals, and taught new farming methods to the peasants.
- They set up communist councils and gave peasants a say in the running of their affairs.
- Class enemies such as rich peasants and landlords were attacked and murdered, and their property seized.
- Hundreds of thousands of class enemies were worked to death or executed under the CCP's *(p.22)* orders.
- Anyone suspected of disloyalty was purged from the party or executed. For example, 200 Red Army soldiers were executed for staging a rebellion against the purges.
- The Red Army used Jiangxi as a base from which to launch guerrilla attacks against the GMD forces opposing them in the civil war.
- During the years 1930-1934, the GMD launched 5 Extermination Campaigns against the CCP *(p.22)* and the Jiangxi Soviet.

What was the outcome of the Jiangxi Soviet?

There were 7 key outcomes as a result of the Jiangxi Soviet:

- Land redistribution gave millions of poor peasants land for the first time. It allowed them to start to climb out of poverty.
- The CCP *(p.22)* won a lot of support due to their reforms and lack of corruption.
- The Red Army grew from just over 10,000 men to over 130,000 by the time of the Long March. The *(p.29)* Red Army was now made up of willing recruits who wanted to fight to defend communism.
- Mao Zedong *(p.31)* had shown his potential as a leader and a general. However, he was still not in overall control of the CCP *(p.22)*.
- Chinese people who were identified as class enemies would never support the communists now, as they knew they could be jailed, tortured or killed for owning land or businesses.
- The Red Army developed tactics to fight a guerrilla war against the much larger and better-equipped GMD forces.
- By 1934, the GMD Extermination Campaigns had killed over 700,000 peasants and resulted in the capture of communist-held towns and villages.

> **DID YOU KNOW?**
>
> **Even within the Jiangxi Soviet you weren't safe!**
> Mao executed nearly 3,000 soldiers in 1930 for not showing complete loyalty to him and for being suspected GMD agents. This became known as the Futian Incident.

THE LONG MARCH

'It is impossible not to recognise the Long March as one of the great triumphs of men against odds and men against nature. While the Red Army was unquestionably in forced retreat, its toughened veterans reached their planned objective with moral and political will as strong as ever…' - Edgar Snow, 1937

What was the Long March?
The Long March was the relocation of 100,000 communists, following the Extermination Campaigns.

When was the Long March?
The Long March took place between the 16th October 1934 and October 1935.

Who was involved in the Long March?
An estimated 100,000 communists relocated.

Where did the Long March go?
The communists marched from Jiangxi to Yanan, in the north of the country.

Why did the Long March happen?
Following the 'White Terror' (the Shanghai Massacres), the communists took refuge in the Jiangxi Soviet *(p.27)*. However, they lost strength and began to steadily retreat as a result of the Extermination Campaigns. By October 1934, it was clear to the communists that they would be destroyed if they remained at the Jiangxi Soviet.

What were the key events of the Long March?
There were 4 key events in the Long March:

- ☑ Upon leaving, the GMD army chased the communists constantly. At first, those travelling suffered huge losses after engaging in battle with the GMD in urban areas.
- ☑ In January 1935, Mao Zedong *(p.31)* and Zhu De became leaders of the CCP *(p.22)*.
- ☑ This led to a reorganisation of tactics; communist groups were subdivided and fought using guerrilla warfare, to avoid directly fighting more powerful GMD forces.
- ☑ The Long March exposed the communists to extremely tough conditions. When they arrived in Yanan, it is estimated only 10% survived.

What was the importance of the Long March?
There were 6 key outcomes from the Long March:

- ☑ It provided superb propaganda and created martyrs, which encouraged others to join the CCP *(p.22)*.

Get our free app at GCSEHistory.com

- Mao became established as the outright leader of the CCP *(p.22)*.
- With only 10,000 survivors, the march promoted the idea of self-sacrifice and set an example for others to follow.
- It provided the CCP *(p.22)* with a stable base area in Yanan, where they could develop policies and support for communism.
- As the CCP *(p.22)*, or "Red Army" went through villages, it gained the support of the people.
- However, the GMD also used this as propaganda, calling the march 'the Great Retreat'. This also seemed to confirm the GMD's control of China, with many western governments now recognising Chiang's government.

DID YOU KNOW?

The marchers had to go to extreme lengths to survive.

With the extreme cold and lack of food on the route to Gansu, some marchers resorted to eating the grain from their companions' excrement.

ZUNYI, 1935

One of the key steps in Mao's rise to power, the Zunyi Conference would help him establish dominance over the CCP.

What was the Zunyi Conference?

The Zunyi Conference was an important meeting between the leaders of the CCP *(p.22)* during the Long March.

Where was the Zunyi Conference held?

The conference was held in the town of Zunyi, in South West China.

When was the Zunyi Conference held?

The Zunyi Conference took place from the 15th to 17th January, 1935.

Who attended the Zunyi Conference?

The conference was attended by key leaders of the CCP *(p.22)* and the Red Army. This included the following 5 people:

- Mao Zedong *(p.31)*, who was only one of several military commanders in the Red Army.
- Bo Gu, who was the leading communist in the CCP *(p.22)* and in overall command.
- Zhu De, who was the overall commander of the Red Army.
- Otto Braun, a German communist, who had been sent by the Soviet Union to advise Bo and Zhu on military tactics.
- Zhou Enlai, who was second-in-command of the Red Army.

Why was the Zunyi Conference held?

After escaping the Jiangxi Soviet *(p.27)*, the CCP *(p.22)* fought at the Battle of Xiang River. There are 2 key reasons the Zunyi Conference would be held after this battle.

- The Red Army had nearly been wiped out at the Battle of Xiang River, after escaping from Jiangxi. In two days of fighting the Red Army lost 40,000 men. At the end of the battle, there were only 35,000 soldiers left.
- The commanders of the Red Army and the CCP *(p.22)* had attacked GMD fortifications head on, based on the advice of Otto Braun, and had suffered terrible casualties.

What signs of tension were there at the Zunyi Conference?

The Zunyi Conference was very tense for 2 key reasons:

- Mao Zedong *(p.31)* used the conference to attack the leadership of Bo Gu and his adviser Otto Braun, who he blamed for the near-destruction of the CCP *(p.22)* at the Battle of Xiang River.
- Bo Gu would not accept any responsibility and supported Otto Braun's advice to fight the GMD in face-to-face battles.

Why was the Zunyi Conference important?

The Zunyi Conference was important for 5 key reasons:

- It became the meeting in which Mao Zedong *(p.31)* openly engaged in a power struggle for control of the CCP *(p.22)*.
- Mao used the meeting to attack his rivals and make himself the obvious choice to take over as leader of the CCP *(p.22)*.
- Bo Gu would not admit to any failure and defended his own leadership.
- Zhou Enlai admitted the Red Army had been mistaken in its tactics.
- Mao Zedong *(p.31)* argued the leadership should be changed and the Red Army should fight a guerrilla war against the GMD.

What decisions were taken at the Zunyi Conference?

There were 5 key decisions at the Zunyi Conference:

- Mao Zedong *(p.31)* was elected as the new leader of the CCP *(p.22)* and overall military commander.
- Mao made it clear he would avoid head-to-head battles with the larger GMD forces.
- Zhou Enlai, second-in-command of the Red Army, was loyal to Mao and promoted to lead the force.
- Bo Gu was demoted and lost power to Mao Zedong *(p.31)*.
- Otto Braun was demoted and would never again be allowed to advise the Red Army.

DID YOU KNOW?

Zunyi tooks years to make it to the history books!

The conference wasn't referenced until the 1950s, and no official history of the conference came from the CCP until 1985.

MAO ZEDONG

'Politics is war without blood, while war is politics with blood.'
Mao Zedong, 1964

Who was Mao Zedong?

Mao Zedong is most famously known as the leading figure in the Chinese Communist Party's *(p.22)* rise and consolidation of power.

When did Mao Zedong live?

Mao was born in 1893 and died in 1976. He ruled China from 1949 until his death.

Where was Mao Zedong born?

Mao was born in Changsha Fu, China.

What was Mao Zedong's role?

Mao Zedong played 3 key roles during his life:

- Mao was an influential Chinese communist revolutionary from the mid-1920s, playing a key role in the August Uprising, the Red Army and the Jiangxi Soviet (p.27).
- He would consolidate his power as leader of the CCP (p.22) during the Long March, later defeating the GMD during the Civil War.
- After victory in the Civil War, Mao would rule the People's Republic China (PRC) from 1949 until his death in 1976.

DID YOU KNOW?

Mao did not brush his teeth!

He washed his mouth out with tea instead. When questioned about this by his doctor, he replied: 'Does a tiger brush his teeth?'

LIFE AT YANAN

Yanan provided the 'holy place for Chinese revolution', where the 'soul of the Chinese nation' was formed, according to an article from newspaper People's Daily in 2013. However, it also saw Mao's consolidation of power and crushing of enemies within the CCP.

What was the Yanan Soviet?

The Yanan Soviet was the new safe area established by the CCP (p.22) at the end of the Long March.

Who was at the Yanan Soviet?

There were 3 main groups that survived the Long March to arrive at the safety of Yanan.

- The First Red Army, commanded by Mao Zedong (p.31), consisted of the few surviving soldiers from the march and their families.
- The Second Red Army reached Yanan after completing its own Long March from Hubei in central China.
- The Fourth Red Army also reached Yanan.

When was the Yanan Soviet established?

The survivors of the Long March arrived in Yanan during October 1935.

Where was the Yanan Soviet?

The Yanan Soviet was established in Shaanxi province of North West China.

What were the key changes in the Yanan Soviet?

There were 4 key changes that resulted from the establishment of the Yanan Soviet:

- The first key change was political. The Yanan Soviet would be governed as a communist state. The CCP (p.22) would rule, but peasants would be given chances to join their own local councils.

- The second key change was in the structure of society. Social equality would be implemented for all residents.
- The third key change was economic. There would be a redistribution of wealth and shared responsibility for production.
- The fourth key change was the adoption of a new approach to fighting the Japanese and the GMD. The Red Army would now fight a guerrilla war in the countryside.

What changes to people's lives happened at Yanan?

Everyday life changed in 8 main ways for people living within the Yanan Soviet:
- A Land Law was implemented that redistributed land from the wealthy estate owners to landless peasants.
- Rents and taxes were abolished or made fairer to allow the poorest peasants to improve their standard of living.
- The Red Army produced thousands of new pieces of farming equipment, and volunteer brigades helped on the farmers' lands.
- Women were provided with new-found freedoms, such as the right to choose whom they married and the right to divorce abusive husbands.
- Brutal and oppressive traditions such as foot binding, infanticide (the murder of female babies), prostitution and the sale of women were outlawed.
- Society was organised along the principal of equality. Communist officials lived and worked alongside the peasants.
- Hospitals, schools and factories were built to provide for the Soviet, and to improve the living standards of the inhabitants.
- There were programmes to address illiteracy and to provide education to all peasants.

What was the significance of the Yanan Soviet?

The Yanan Soviet was significant for 7 key reasons:
- The Red Army had been reduced from 100,000 to 10,000 men and Communist Party membership had fallen from 300,000 to around 40,000. However, Yanan would enable the communists to recover their strength.
- Yanan enabled Mao Zedong *(p.31)* to establish supreme power over the Communist Party.
- It was at Yanan that the cult of Mao was established. The influence of his political writings and destruction of all opposition voices in the party was so great that Chinese communism became 'Maoism'.
- Mao won over the peasants with his political, social and economic policies. Acting less harshly than at Jiangxi proved to the Chinese people the communists could make their lives better.
- The Red Army lived by Mao's rules of Red Army Discipline that prevented them from harming the peasants or their possessions. This won them the support of the peasants in their fight against the Japanese and the GMD.
- Yanan was a great propaganda success as it proved to the people of China there was an alternative government to the GMD and a better way of life under communism.
- Mao became so revered at Yanan that he was called the 'Great Helmsman' in recognition of his importance as the leader of Chinese communism.

DID YOU KNOW?

Yanan has distinctive yellow soil.
Known as loess, it is incredibly rich and created by an accumulation of wind-blown dust.

XIAN INCIDENT, 1936

The Xian Incident saw the kidnap of Chiang Kai-shek and was an important moment in Chinese 20th century history, as the GMD's attention was forcibly turned towards the Japanese.

What was the Xian Incident?
The Xian Incident was the event that forced the GMD to form a 'Second United Front' with the CCP *(p.22)*.

When was the Xian Incident?
The Xian Incident took place between the 12th and 24th December, 1936.

Who was involved in the Xian Incident?
There were 3 key people involved in the Xian Incident:
- Zhang Xueliang, or the 'Young Marshall,' was a powerful warlord and ruler of north-eastern China. He was an ally of the GMD.
- Chiang Kai-shek *(p.21)* was the President of China and commander of all GMD and allied forces.
- Zhou Enlai was Mao Zedong's *(p.31)* second in command and vice-Chairman of the CCP *(p.22)*.

What happened during the Xian Incident?
There were 5 key events during the Xian Incident:
- In 1936 Chiang Kai-shek *(p.21)* was planning a final offensive against the CCP *(p.22)*.
- In December 1936, Chiang flew to Zhang Xueliang's headquarters in northern China to lead the offensive.
- Zhang refused to attack the CCP *(p.22)* and demanded Chiang fight the Japanese instead. As a result, Zhang took Chiang hostage.
- Zhang forced Chiang to meet with Zhou Enlai in order to come to an agreement with the CCP *(p.22)*.
- Zhou and Chiang agreed a ceasefire between the GMD and the CCP *(p.22)*. Chiang promised to form a 'Second United Front' against Japan. Zhou promised Chiang the CCP would accept his leadership.

Why did the Xian Incident happen?
There were 5 important reasons for the Xian Incident:
- Chiang Kai-shek *(p.21)* was focused on destroying the CCP *(p.22)*, rather than the Japanese occupation of Manchuria. He said the Japanese were 'a disease of the skin', whereas communism was 'a disease of the heart', meaning Japan was less of a threat than the CCP.
- Zhang Xueliang, the 'Young Marshall', had been ordered to destroy the CCP *(p.22)* operating from their base at Jiangxi in northern China.
- Zhang's father had been assassinated by the Japanese and his Northern Army came from the regions occupied by Japan. They had strong nationalist feelings and felt Japan was the greater threat.
- Japan occupied Manchuria and it was well known the Japanese were preparing an invasion into northern China.
- Zhang had entered into talks with the CCP *(p.22)* to try to form an anti-Japanese alliance before Chiang arrived at his headquarters.

What was significant about the Xian Incident?
The Xian Incident was significant for 5 reasons:
- It ended the first phase of the civil war between the GMD and the CCP *(p.22)*.
- The incident secured time for Mao Zedong *(p.31)* to recover from GMD attacks and build the fighting strength of the CCP's *(p.22)* Red Army.
- The formation of the Second United Front established the CCP *(p.22)* as a credible nationalist force, willing to fight the Japanese. Chiang Kai-shek's *(p.21)* reputation was undermined.

- ✅ Chiang never intended to keep to the agreement as he had been forced into it. There would only be a short break in hostilities between the GMD and the CCP *(p.22)*.
- ✅ The Soviet Union recognised Chiang Kai-shek *(p.21)* as leader of the Second United Front and agreed to supply his forces with arms to fight Japan.

> **DID YOU KNOW?**
>
> **Xian was one of China's ancient capitals.**
> Xian was the capital during the Zhou, Qin, Han, Sui, and Tang dynasties. Today, it is home to the Terracotta Army.

JAPANESE INVASION OF CHINA, 1937

Following a skirmish on the border, Japan would invade China and spark the beginnings of the Second World War. This would again unite the GMD and CCP in a fight against the foreign invader.

What was the Japanese invasion of China?
In 1937, an incident between Japanese and Chinese soldiers took place which quickly escalated into a full-scale war.

When did the Japan invasion of China begin?
The incident took place on the night of July 8th, 1937.

Where did the invasion of China by Japan begin?
The spark that prompted the Japanese invasion of China began as an incident on the Marco Polo Bridge, located in Wanping, 15 kilometres from Beijing.

Who fought in Japan's invasion of China?
The incident occured between Chinese troops guarding the Marco Polo Bridge, and Japanese troops who were in the area searching for a missing soldier.

Why did the Japanese invasion of China happen?
The Marco Polo Bridge Incident was an accident which soon led to war for 4 reasons:
- ✅ The Chinese controlled the bridge but the Japanese controlled the territory around it. Tensions between the two sides were high.
- ✅ It was night, and it is believed a nervous Chinese sentry fired a shot at nearby Japanese soldiers, believing an attack was under way.
- ✅ The Japanese launched a series of full-scale attacks against Chinese garrisons in Beijing and Tianjin.
- ✅ The Imperial Japanese Army (IJA) already had plans to invade China and used the incident as an excuse to put them into action.

What were the key events of Japan's invasion of China?
There were 3 key events that resulted from the Marco Polo Bridge Incident:
- ✅ It quickly became a good reason for the Japanese military to put its invasion plan into effect, and seize more territory and resources from China.
- ✅ In the weeks following the Marco Polo Bridge Incident, the Japanese surrounded and occupied Beijing.

- The Japanese headed south until they could surround and besiege Shanghai, China's most important port city.

Why was the invasion of China by Japan significant?

The Marco Polo Bridge Incident and invasion of China was significant for 6 key reasons:

- The Marco Polo Bridge Incident began the Second Sino-Japanese War *(p.36)*, which would last until 1945.
- The Second Sino-Japanese War *(p.36)* would last eight years and become part of the Second World War in Asia.
- The invasion united the Chinese people in defence of their country.
- More Japanese troops would fight in China throughout the conflict than fought against either the Americans in the Pacific, or the British Empire in Southeast Asia.
- The conflict would provide an opportunity for the CCP *(p.22)* and the Red Army to increase their territory, experience and support.
- The GMD would be weakened as it would do most of the fighting throughout the conflict.

> **DID YOU KNOW?**
>
> **The Marco Polo Bridge is actually known as the Lugou Bridge in China!**
>
> It became known as the Marco Polo Bridge after he visited and praised it in his 13th century book of travels.

THE WAR WITH JAPAN, 1937-45

'You must all be aware that modern war is not a mere matter of military operations. It involves the whole strength and resources of the nation. Not only soldiers, but all citizens without exception, take part.'
Chiang Kai-shek.

What was the war between China and Japan?

This was a war between China and Japan, fought over Chinese territory which Japan had invaded. It is also known as the Second Sino-Japanese War.

When was the Japanese War?

The war began in July 1937 and ended in September 1945.

Who fought in the Japanese War?

The Chinese forces consisted of both the GMD and the CCP *(p.22)*. This became known as the Second United Front. The Second United Front then fought against the Imperial Japanese Army.

Why did the Japanese War begin?

The war began as a result of the Japanese invasion of China *(p.35)*, and occurred for 5 main reasons:

- After the invasion of Manchuria in 1931, Japan had continued to consolidate its position in China. From 1937, Japan began to expand to other regions.
- At first, Chiang had allowed this to occur as he was more concerned with the fight against the communists. However, warlords became concerned at this policy and petitioned Chiang to remove the Japanese.
- Due to this pressure, Chiang forced an alliance with the communists called the Second United Front with the goal of removing Japanese influence in China.

What were the key events of the Japanese War?

There were 7 key events in the war with Japan:

- July 1937: Chiang declared war against Japan.
- July 1937-December 1937: There were major losses across the north east of China, with Japan taking control across the area through to Shanghai. It also gained control of Guangzhou in the south.
- December 1937: The Rape of Nanking. Defeat looked imminent, with 30,000 Chinese soldiers killed, and an estimated 20,000 women raped during the battle for Nanjing, the GMD capital.
- December 1937 onwards: China reverted to guerrilla warfare, with the Red Army having huge success. New recruits and the new tactics provided resistance against the Japanese.
- May 1941: The Allies begin to supply China with sending Lend-Lease supplies and resources for their fight against Japan.
- December 1941: Japan bombed the US naval base at Pearl Harbour. Due to the attack, China became one of the wartime Allies along with the USA, Great Britain and the Soviet Union. China recieved more men and supplies from the Allies.
- August 1945: Japan was heavily weakened after years of Allied attacks on its main islands. The war ended following the dropping of the atomic bombs on Japan.

What was the CCP's role in the Japanese War?

The CCP *(p.22)* played an important role supplying vital troops and launching the Hundred Regiments Offensive in 1940. This, plus guerrilla warfare, halted the Japanese invasion.

What was the GMD's role in the Japanese War?

The GMD suffered heavily during the war due to a preoccupation with undermining the communists, rather than fighting the Japanese. Due to recruitment tactics and the limited impact it had on the war, public support for the GMD decreased.

What impact did the Second World War have on China and the war with Japan?

The Second World War affected China in 11 ways:

- The Second Sino-Japanese War began with the invasion of China in 1937 and became part of the Second World War in December 1941, after Britain and the USA were attacked by Japan.
- China became one of the main allied nations in the Second World War by declaring war on Japan, Germany and Italy days after the USA declared war on Japan.
- China was a key ally and became one of the Big Four, along with the USA, Britain and the Soviet Union. This intensified the war in China, as Japan became increasingly desperate to force China to surrender.
- In 1944, the Japanese began their largest offensive of the Second World War. They used over 500,000 men in Operation Ichi-Go to try and destroy American airfields in China and link up with their forces occupying Vietnam.
- The Japanese adopted a scorched earth policy in China called the 'Three Alls Campaign': 'Kill all, burn all, loot all.' These campaigns were directed against China's civilian population and killed millions.
- The USA and the Soviet Union recognised Chiang Kai-shek *(p.21)* as President of the Republic of China and supplied large amounts of arms and equipment to nationalist forces.
- In 1945, China under Chiang, was recognised as one of the victorious allied powers. However, at least 25 million Chinese people had died.
- By 1945, the Chinese economy had been destroyed and there was severe inflation.
- The Second United Front had collapsed in 1941 and, by 1945, China was already in the early stages of another period of civil war.
- The CCP *(p.22)* had increased its territory and communist China was now more popular than nationalist China.
- By 1945, the CCP *(p.22)* were skilled fighters and party membership numbered over 1.2 million.

> **DID YOU KNOW?**
>
> **The Qing dynasty tried to make a comeback!**
> Emperor Puyi, who was now in his mid-20s, had a failed attempt to become emperor again with Japanese support. He left China, returning in 1949 to live as a member of the general population.

THE CIVIL WAR, 1946-49

'Thousands upon thousands of martyrs have heroically laid down their lives for the people; let us hold their banner high and march ahead along the path crimson with their blood!'
Mao Zedong, April 1945

What was the Chinese Civil War?
The Chinese Civil War was a conflict between the GMD and the CCP *(p.22)* for control of China.

Who was involved in the Chinese Civil War?
The GMD faced off against the CCP *(p.22)* with their respective armies. This was similar to the situation before the war against Japan began in 1937.

When did the Chinese Civil War take place?
The civil war lasted from July 1946 to October 1949. Unofficially, some would argue this actually began in 1927 and was only paused because of the war with Japan.

Why did the Chinese Civil War happen?
Once the war against Japan had ended, the Allies backed Chiang's attempt to seize power by establishing a GMD dominated government. This angered the communists and no agreement could be made, leading to fighting and the continuation of the civil war.

What were the key phases of the Chinese Civil War?
There were 3 key phases to the Chinese Civil War:
- ☑ July 1946-May 1947: The GMD controlled the majority of the north including capturing Yanan. However, using the newly named People's Liberation Army (PLA), the CCP *(p.22)* employed guerrilla warfare to take control of northern Manchuria.
- ☑ May 1947-November 1948: The PLA changed tactics and used conventional warfare to attack the GMD directly. The PLA pushed forward into the western territories with the northern areas consolidated under communist rule.
- ☑ December 1948-October 1949: Conventional warfare continued and huge battles, such as the Battle of Huaihai *(p.39)*, take place. Both sides suffered major losses before the GMD forces began to collapse. The communists then pushed on to secure overall victory.

What were the key outcomes of the Chinese Civil War?
There were 4 key outcomes of the Chinese Civil War:
- ☑ By October 1949, the majority of China was under communist control.
- ☑ Mao declared himself leader of the People's Republic of China (PRC).
- ☑ The GMD leadership fled China with Chiang Kai-shek *(p.21)*, relocating their government to Taiwan.

- It is estimated the civil war cost the lives of 2.5 million people, including 750,000 civilians.

What were the reasons for communist victory in the Chinese Civil War?

There were 5 reasons the CCP *(p.22)* won the civil war:

- Military leadership: Mao created an in-depth plan to win the war with skilled generals who executed it well.
- Military tactics: Mao's army was dynamic and employed different tactics to suit each situation. The use of both guerrilla warfare and conventional warfare is evidence of this.
- Quality of troops: Mao's army showed extreme discipline and this gained the support of the peasants, who were badly treated by the GMD.
- Political: Mao marketed communism well, with propaganda showing united leadership and democratic dictatorship. This attracted a lot of support.
- Economic/social: Mao introduced land reform which benefitted the peasants, and in turn, secured their loyalty. The CCP *(p.22)* was also seen as more nationalistic as they had always opposed and resisted the Japanese.

What were the reasons for GMD defeat in the Chinese Civil War?

There were 5 reasons the GMD lost the civil war:

- Military leadership: Chiang Kai-shek *(p.21)* was inexperienced and demanded full control. He wouldn't give his generals freedom to make decisions.
- Military tactics: The GMD made huge tactical blunders. They attacked on numerous occasions without securing a supply line, leaving themselves isolated. Likewise, they did not respond well to the different tactics employed by the PLA.
- Quality of troops: The National Revolutionary Army was formed by forced conscription, and fought with limited supplies and harsh punishments. Deaths and desertions were high, which led to a reduction in the strength of the army.
- Political: Chiang was beginning to lose the support of the people. His corruption and abuse of power had left the GMD in an unfavourable position.
- Economic/social: Chiang created a currency crisis when he printed more money to fund the government. This impacted the middle class in particular, who were some of his key supporters. Despite attempts to solve the issues with a new currency, Chiang lost the support of the people.

DID YOU KNOW?

While Mao won the civil war, the GMD did not help itself!

In GMD areas, many people turned to crime as the currency had no value. There were strikes and rebellions against the GMD and many saw the communists as their only chance of survival.

THE BATTLE OF HUAIHAI

The Battle of Huaihai would act as one of the GMD's final defences. Following this battle, it was resigned to defeat and the birth of Mao's China could begin.

What was the Battle of Huaihai?

The Battle of Huaihai was a key battle during the Chinese Civil War *(p.38)*.

Who fought in the Battle of Huaihai?

The National Revolutionary Army (NRA) fought against the People's Liberation Army (PLA) during this battle. It is estimated the NRA numbered 800,000 compared to the PLA's 600,000.

When was the Battle of Huaihai?

The Battle of Huaihai took place between 6th November, 1948 and 10th January, 1949.

Where was the Battle of Huaihai?

The Battle of Huaihai took place in a number of central and eastern provinces - Henan, Jiangsu, Shandong and Anhui.

What were the outcomes from the Battle of Huaihai?

There were 4 key outcomes from the battle:

- Chiang Kai-shek *(p.21)* surrendered on 10th January, 1949 after huge losses totalling 200,000 men.
- The defeat opened up central China to communist control.
- It marked the end of funding for Chiang's government from Allied forces.
- It signalled the collapse of the NRA and put the PLA firmly in control of the civil war.

DID YOU KNOW?

It was one of the few conventional battles of the war.

Before this point, there was a lot of focus on guerrilla tactics, which meant smaller battles and fewer casualties.

AGRARIAN REFORM LAW, 1950

With Civil War behind them, Mao went about his work in creating a communist China. His first reforms would focus on agricultural society.

What was the Agrarian Reform Law?

The Agrarian Reform Law was the reorganisation of land ownership in order to enforce the policy of collectivisation.

What were the aims of the Agrarian Reform Law?

There were 2 main aims of the Agrarian Reform Law:

- To remove the property of large landlords and redistribute it among the peasants.
- To confiscate the property of any foreigners or enemies of China, such as Chiang Kai-shek *(p.21)*.

Why was the Agrarian Reform Law introduced?

Reform was introduced for 2 reasons:

- Reform was needed in order to centralise and improve food production in the countryside, allowing surplus workers to take up industrial work in the towns.
- Mao Zedong *(p.31)* believed larger landlords were exploiting peasants at the expense of his communist system.

What were the outcomes of the Agrarian Reform Law?

There were 4 outcomes from the law:

- 1 million landlords were executed.
- Thousands were sent to be re-educated with communist ideology.
- The law allowed for the removal of the Chinese elite and redistribution of wealth to the peasants, which was extremely popular among the peasants.
- It allowed for the collectivisation of agriculture to begin.

DID YOU KNOW?

The new law named and shamed!

The law ordered that land be confiscated from the 'four big families' of the GMD - the Kungs, Soongs, Chiangs and Chens.

MARRIAGE LAW, 1950

'Under feudal domination, marriage is a barbaric and inhuman institution. The oppression and suffering born by women is far greater than that of man. Only the victory of the workers' and peasants' revolution... brings with it a change in the marriage relationship and makes it free.'
Mao Zedong, 1931

What was the Marriage Law?

The Marriage Law was a series of reforms to the laws of marriage in China.

When was the Marriage Law introduced?

The Marriage Law was introduced in 1950, a year into the First Five Year Plan.

Why was the Marriage Law introduced?

Before the Marriage Law, women did not have equal rights and were treated as being lesser than men. For Mao's communist society to succeed, he needed to ensure everyone was seen as equal.

What were the key features of the Marriage Law?

The Marriage Law outlined 6 requirements:

- Arranged marriages were banned, along with dowries. If you were in an arranged marriage, then you were given the opportunity to divorce.
- The age of marriage was raised. Males had to be 20 years old and females 18 years old in order to get married.
- It was forbidden for men to have mistresses as well as a wife.
- Divorce rights were made accessible and equal to both men and women.
- Women were given equal property rights, allowing them to buy and sell property.
- Infanticide was banned. This was a particular issue with baby girls as, under the previous system, they were seen as expensive due to marriage dowry payments.

> **DID YOU KNOW?**
>
> **Mao had his own arranged marriage!**
> Mao had an arranged married to his cousin Luo Yixiu. However, Mao refused to live with his new bride as he was so opposed to the practice.

THE COLLECTIVISATION OF AGRICULTURE

'More than 60 million peasant households in various parts of the country have already joined the cooperatives. It is as if a raging tidal wave has swept away all the demons and ghosts.' Mao Zedong, 1955.

What was Chinese collectivisation?

Collectivisation was the reorganisation of land into one mass, which could be farmed as a community, rather than by individuals.

What were the stages of Chinese collectivisation?

There were 4 main stages of collectivisation under Mao:

- At first, peasants were encouraged to form mutual aid teams of up to 10 households. However, only 40% of peasants had taken up this option up by the end of 1952.
- From 1953, Mao encouraged the formation of Agricultural Producers' Co-operatives (APCs). These were made up of up to 5 mutual aid teams and allowed for an increase in efficiency.
- The APC scheme was successful, though some richer peasants took advantage of the scheme. They used it to purchase large sections of lands and hired peasants to work on them. This created resistance from the peasants and a process of forced labour took place, finally leading to this policy being paused in January 1955.
- The final stage was the introduction of collectives. These consisted of up to 3,000 households with no private ownership. By 1958, 700 million peasants were in a collective farm.

What were the results of Chinese collectivisation?

While Mao had achieved his goal of increased food output and stimulated a demand for machinery, success was short-lived due to the Great Famine that emerged in 1958.

> **DID YOU KNOW?**
>
> **Mao was protected from the true reality of his policies!**
> When Mao travelled through China by train, it was arranged for crops to be brought and placed alongside the track. This meant Mao would think the policy was a great success. Once he had passed, the crops were returned.

THE FIRST FIVE YEAR PLAN, 1952-57

Rapid modernisation and movement away from the agrarian model was needed to push China forward. The First Five Year Plan was an attempt by Mao and the CCP to achieve this.

What was China's First Five Year Plan?

This was plan to modernise China by developing its industry.

When did China's First Five Year Plan run?

The First Five Year Plan ran from 1952 to 1957.

What were the aims of China's First Five Year Plan?

The plan's focus was on the expansion of heavy industry within China. This would include production of iron, petroleum, steel and coal.

What were the outcomes of China's First Five Year Plan?

There were 4 impressive outcomes from the First Five Year Plan:

- Production of coal doubled during the period.
- Steel production increased four-fold during the period.
- Electrical output increased three-fold during the period.
- The plan was so successful it led to a second plan, more commonly known as the Great Leap Forward *(p.43)*.

DID YOU KNOW?

All with a little help from my friend...
The Soviets were influential in helping China develop its own five year plan.

THE GREAT LEAP FORWARD, 1958-62

'I suggest that we bestow upon the scientist or scientists who invented this great slogan, 'Leap Forward', the title of First Doctor of Philosophy!'
Mao Zedong, 1957

What was the Great Leap Forward?

The Great Leap Forward was the Second Five Year Plan, which aimed to continue the modernisation of China's industry and make it a world power.

Who introduced the Great Leap Forward?

The plan was introduced by Liu Shaoqi on behalf of the People's Republic of China and the Chinese Communist Party *(p.22)*.

When was the Great Leap Forward?

The plan was launched in May 1958 and ran until 1962.

Why was the Great Leap Forward introduced?

There were 5 reasons the Great Leap Forward was introduced:

- Mao wanted to continue the progress China had made in the First Five Year Plan.
- Collectivisation, both fed the workforce, and provided a surplus that was exported and used to fund industry.
- There was a genuine belief that socialism was the system of governance to follow in light of the Soviet Union's achievements, such as victories in the space race.
- Mao wanted to be self-sufficient and not rely on foreign interests or influence, especially from the Soviet Union.
- Mao was headstrong and believed anything was possible.

What were the key features of the Great Leap Forward?

The Great Leap Forward had 5 key features:

- Huge projects were commissioned to help drive industry forwards. Projects such as bridges, canals and dams were all constructed during this period.
- All private business came under state control, allowing for greater command over production.
- There was a huge drive behind steel production, so much so that 600,000 'backyard furnaces' were set up in family backyards.
- The move from APCs to full collectivisation was confirmed and enforced. This allowed control over the supply of food to workers.
- It involved the whole population. The Great Leap Forward utilised all workers to reach common goals.

What were the effects of the Great Leap Forward?

The Great Leap Forward had a fairly poor outcome. It had 6 important effects, most of which were failures:

- Success: Production increased in all areas. Coal saw the biggest output, peaking at around 300 million tonnes in 1960.
- Failure: Collectivisation was one reason for the Great Famine, in which 50 million people died.
- Failure: Steel production from 'backyard furnaces' was of poor quality and couldn't be used.
- Failure: Wider business production decreased due to state ownership. The lack of profit motivation meant there was no desire to produce.
- Failure: As Mao wanted to distance China from Soviet influence, he allowed the Soviet experts to leave the country before China was in a position to replace and operate without them.
- Failure: Mao resigned as head of state and was humiliated. He went into hiding and made few public appearances.

DID YOU KNOW?

The failure of the Great Leap Forward is still recognised in China today.

The Great Famine and the Great Leap Forward period is known as the 'Three Years of Natural Disasters' or the 'Three Years of Difficulties'.

THE GREAT FAMINE, 1958-62

'When there is not enough to eat, people starve to death. It is better to let half of the people die so that the other half can eat their fill.'
Mao Zedong, 1959.

What was the Chinese Great Famine?
The Chinese Great Famine was a period of limited food supply in China which killed 50 million people.

Why did the Chinese Great Famine happen?
There were 5 reasons behind the Great Famine:
- ✓ Lack of incentives: Due to collectivisation, peasants no longer sold excess stock for profit so there was no incentive to grow more or attain higher yields.
- ✓ Four Pests Campaign: Mao had launched a campaign to remove 'pests' which ate agricultural produce. However, by disturbing the ecosystem, more crops were eaten by wildlife.
- ✓ Political influence: Mao used guidance from Soviet scientists who believed their methods would increase crop yields more than 16 times over. However, this proved incorrect.
- ✓ Fear: People did not want to speak out about the failure to produce enough food as they feared repercussions.
- ✓ Natural events: China had suffered a drought which limited harvested goods.

What was the result of the Chinese Great Famine?
Up to 50 million people died as a result of the famine. It also caused families to be separated as parents were forced to swap their children for food items. Tibet in particular suffered, with more than 1 million people dying.

DID YOU KNOW?

We will never know the true extent of damage caused by the Great Famine.

Historians have estimated anywhere between 16.5 to 45 million individuals died. If it were 45 million, that would be the equivalent of two thirds of the British population today.

CHANGES IN THE ROLE OF WOMEN

As Mao came to power, he saw modernising the role of women as vital to China's success. Policies across politics, marriage and the economy were implemented to varying success.

What were the changes in policy towards women from 1950 to 1962?
There were a number of changes in China's policy towards women between the years 1950 and 1962 due to the Marriage Law *(p.41)* and other initiatives.

What areas did the 1950-1962 policy changes towards women cover?
These changes can be categorised into 4 key areas:
- ✓ Marriage.
- ✓ Family.
- ✓ Economics.

- Politics.

What impact did the 1950-1962 policy changes towards women have on marriage?

There was a mixed response, with 4 main impacts in relation to marriage:

- Many opposed the Marriage Law *(p.41)*, especially in the heavily Muslim west. This led to arranged marriages continuing.
- The exchanging of gifts and dowries continued in rural areas.
- Divorce, though legal, was seen to bring shame upon a family.
- There was some success, as the average age of marriage rose and the number of infanticides reduced.

What impact did the 1950-1962 policy changes towards women have on family life?

Policies towards family life brought about 2 positive changes:

- China produced contraceptives, allowing for autonomy of choice and helping reduce the rate of infanticide. There was resistance to this, however, particularly in rural areas.
- Childbirth became a safer process, with better training and standardised procedures.

What impact did the 1950-1962 policy changes towards women have on women's economic roles?

The impact on women's economic roles during this period was also mixed. 4 key changes were:

- The percentage of women working increased to nearly 30% in the 1960s. This was compared to just 8% in 1949.
- Education was more accessible to women, and female literacy rates rose.
- However, property rights were soon withdrawn as collectivisation removed all privately owned property.
- Due to extreme conditions during the Great Famine, men still sold their wives for income which was evidence equality of the sexes had not been achieved.

What impact did the 1950-1962 policy changes toward women have on women's political roles?

Politically, women saw 3 main successes during this period due to Mao's reforms:

- Representation in the Central People's Political Consultative Committee increased. This was reflected in the National People's Congress which also saw a rise.
- While there was some minor opposition to women's involvement in politics, most accepted that women could hold minor roles in government.
- There were some huge successes and role models produced during this period. The elected Ministers for Health and Justice were both women, and showed more fully the intention to integrate women in politics.

DID YOU KNOW?

Mao offered to send 10 million women to the US!

In 1973, Mao was worried about sustaining the population of China. So he offered to trade the women with the USA, saying his country had too many of them.

POLITICAL CHANGES UNDER MAO

Political restructuring took place across China in order to allow Mao to utilise his power and control. While not always at the centre of political happenings, Mao was always pulling the party's strings and dealt with any opposition.

What political changes did Mao make?
While China appeared to be democratic, Mao carefully crafted a system of government which allowed for complete control over the Communist Party and the people.

How did the structure of government change following Mao's political changes?
There were 7 key elements to his new structured system of government:

- Head of CCP/State *(p.22)*: This position was established for Mao and dominated all other elements of the new system of government.
- Politburo: This had a committee of 5 members who were carefully selected by Mao Zedong *(p.31)* and were often his allies within the CCP *(p.22)*. The Politburo governed China under Mao's authority.
- Central Committee of the Party: This comprised 44 members of the CCP *(p.22)* and was usually populated with the party's top leaders.
- State Council of the National Government: This was led by a Premier and carried out administrative and legislative functions for review by the Politburo and Mao.
- The People's Liberation Army: The armed forces for the country and the CCP *(p.22)*.
- National government: This comprised 24 ministries which controlled and standardised aspects of society for the whole country, e.g. banks and education.
- Provincial government: There were 6 regional governments which addressed the needs of the provinces within their areas. Local economic development might be discussed or an external leader inserted to ensure compliance.

DID YOU KNOW?

China had its own war on drugs under Mao.
Mao halted production of opium. He put 10 million users into compulsory treatment and executed anyone found dealing drugs.

MAO ZEDONG THOUGHT

Mao Zedong Thought (Maoism) was Mao's interpretation of communism. Based on Marxism and Leninism but adapted to meet Chinese conditions and ideals, this was Mao's blueprint for the future of communist China.

What was the Mao Zedong Thought?
This was the belief system that Mao used to transform all aspects of society.

What were the key beliefs of the Mao Zedong Thought?
Mao Zedong Thought consisted of 4 key beliefs:

- Prevent opposition and counter-revolution.
- Engage the people through the principle of mass mobilisation.
- Promote the idea of constant class struggle.

✓ Independence and self-reliance, in particular from external influences such as the Soviet Union.

DID YOU KNOW?

Mao was a school dropout!
Mao dropped out of no fewer than 5 different schools before reverting to independent study.

THOUGHT REFORM

'The communist revolution is a total revolution aiming to establish a new society and a new way of life. A new society presupposes new men with new minds, new ideas, new emotions, and new attitudes.'
Theodore Chen, 1969.

What was the Thought Reform Campaign?
The Thought Reform Campaign was a campaign to remove opposition to the CCP *(p.22)* from within China.

Who did the Thought Reform Campaign target?
The targets for the Thought Reform Campaign were intellectuals (who had foreign education), businessmen and party members who strayed from the Mao Zedong Thought *(p.47)*.

Why was the Thought Reform Campaign introduced?
While Mao had removed the majority of GMD opposition, he still believed there was internal opposition that could cause problems for the CCP *(p.22)* in the long term. Therefore, he planned to remove this opposition and consolidate his power.

When was the Thought Reform Campaign introduced?
The two main policies for the Thought Reform Campaign were brought out in 1951 and 1952. The policies remained in place until 1957.

What were the main policies of the Thought Reform Campaign?
There were two main policies of the Thought Reform Campaign:
✓ The Three-anti Campaign, 1951 *(p.49)*.
✓ The Five-anti Campaign *(p.49)*, 1952.

What were the outcomes of the Thought Reform Campaign?
Both the Three and Five-anti Campaigns were highly successful. There were 4 main outcomes:
✓ Numerous people were denounced, with punishments ranging from fines to labour camp sentences.
✓ It is also estimated 3 million people committed suicide due to the embarrassment of public confessions.
✓ Increased support for the CCP *(p.22)* was recorded.
✓ There was also a reduction in criminal activity.

DID YOU KNOW?

Thought Reform had another name.

It was also known as 'sīxiǎng gǎizào', which translated as ideological remoulding or reform.

THE THREE-ANTI CAMPAIGN, 1951

'Where do correct ideas come from? Do they drop from the skies? No. Are they innate in the mind? No. They come from social practice and from it alone.'
Mao Zedong, 1963

What was the Three-anti Campaign?

The Three-anti Campaign was a campaign to remove opposition to Mao during the Thought Reform *(p.48)* Campaign.

When was the Three-anti Campaign launched?

The campaign was launched in 1951.

Who did the Three-anti Campaign target?

The campaign targeted CCP *(p.22)* members and officials working with governmental departments.

What were the Three-anti Campaign aims?

The campaign wanted to fight deceit, waste and a lack of productivity.

DID YOU KNOW?

Enemies of the state were depicted as tigers!

In the propaganda which promoted the campaign, corrupt officials were shown as tigers. Mao encouraged the 'tiger-hunting teams' to 'cleanse away the filth and poison left over in our country from the old society.'

THE FIVE-ANTI CAMPAIGN, 1952

Following the Three-anti Campaign and as part of the wider Thought Reform, the Five-anti Campaign looked to address corruption and enemies of the revolution.

What was the Five-anti Campaign?

The Five-anti Campaign was a campaign to remove business opposition to Mao during the Thought Reform *(p.48)* Campaign.

When was the Five-anti Campaign launched?

The campaign was launched in 1952.

Who did the Five-anti Campaign target?

The campaign targeted businessmen.

What were the Five-anti Campaign aims?

The campaign wanted to fight fraud, theft, tax evasion, bribery and sabotage.

DID YOU KNOW?

The systems created a society of suspicion.

As people were encouraged and praised for speaking out against their family, friends and neighbours, this created a system of suspicion among the general population. In some cases, children even reported on their parents.

THE HUNDRED FLOWERS CAMPAIGN, 1957

'Let a hundred flowers bloom, and a hundred schools of thought contend.'
Mao, 1956.

What was the Hundred Flowers Campaign?

The Hundred Flowers Campaign was a policy to encourage free speech and expression on opinions of the communist regime in China.

When was the Hundred Flowers Campaign?

The campaign began unofficially in May 1956, before being formally introduced in spring 1957.

Why was the Hundred Flowers Campaign introduced?

There were 4 reasons behind Mao's decision to relax censorship and encourage free speech:

- Mao wanted to encourage intellectual freedom in order to restart scientific advancement. Since the Soviets had left, progress in science and technology had slowed.
- Mao also wanted to use this as an opportunity to identify disloyal CCP *(p.22)* members.
- The Hungarian Uprising of 1956 had highlighted the dangers of having limited support from the people. Mao wanted to listen to, and address concerns.
- With Khrushchev taking power in the Soviet Union and criticising Stalin's rule in the 'Secret Speech', Mao wanted to ensure he avoided such comparisons and criticisms.

What were the consequences of the Hundred Flowers Campaign?

There 4 significant consequences to emerge from the Hundred Flowers Campaign:

- The campaign was abruptly halted following criticism of Mao and other CCP *(p.22)* officials. He had thought it would raise trivial issues, rather than direct criticism.
- Mao launched a counter Anti-Rightist Campaign, which labelled critics as enemies and enforced harsh punishments such as re-education on them. Eventually, 750,000 CCP *(p.22)* members were sentenced to receive punishments.

- Mao replaced Peng Dehuai, who had voiced concern over the Great Famine.
- Mao also removed himself as head of state. This allowed him to retain control of the CCP *(p.22)* but also separated him from any failures by the CCP and the state.

DID YOU KNOW?

Mao was all for the movement to begin with and wanted to help further communism in China.

'From my point of view…there are times when nothing but a beating can solve the problem. The CCP has to learn its lesson…and not allow a bureaucratic lifestyle to develop.' Mao, 1956

SINO-SOVIET RELATIONS, 1949-62

'It was Mao's way of putting himself in an advantageous position. Well, I got sick of it…. I crawled out, sat on the edge, and dangled my legs in the pool. Now I was on top and he was swimming below.'
Khrushchev on his swimming meeting with Mao

What were Sino-Soviet relations like between 1949-62?

China and the USSR had mutual interests and ideologies which led to cooperation and collaboration. However, there was a level of mistrust between the powers which grew over time.

What was the Treaty of Friendship in the Sino-Soviet relations?

The Treaty of Friendship was a formal recognition of relations between the Soviet Union and China.

What were the Treaty of Friendship's terms for Sino-Soviet relations?

The Treaty of Friendship included 4 important terms:
- The USSR would aid and support the PRC in the event of an attack or invasion.
- The PRC would receive a loan from the USSR for $300 million.
- The disclosure of all Soviet intelligence agents working in China.
- China also gave economic grants to lands in Manchuria and Xinjiang. However, these were kept secret in order to avoid protests, as this would show Mao and the CCP *(p.22)* acting hypocritically.

What was the Soviet influence on economic developments in Sino-Soviet relations?

There were 3 positive influences that Soviet relations had on Chinese economic development:
- The Soviet loan helped China pay for 10,000 military and economic advisers. These advisers would play significant roles in the First Five Year Plan.
- Under Khrushchev, China was offered trade packages and nuclear support, as well as the Soviets moving out of Manchuria.
- Because of the training and support offered, China was able to build its own nuclear reactor and develop its first nuclear warhead in 1960.

What was the Soviet influence on political developments in Sino-Soviet relations?

Political influence was limited due to strained Sino-Soviet relations, which had deteriorated over time for 3 reasons:
- Mao had a strong distrust of Stalin. After charging excessive amounts in payment for Soviet weapons during the Korean War, Mao believed Stalin was out to weaken and subjugate China.

- With Khrushchev's 'Secret Speech' and criticism of Stalin, Mao felt his style of government and regime was also being criticised. However, after this point Mao Zedong Thought *(p.47)* did become a less important policy for the politburo.
- Despite attempts to improve relations, during the Moscow Conference of 1958, China accused the Soviets of spying and betraying the communist movement.

> **DID YOU KNOW?**
>
> **Relations were not going swimmingly...**
>
> Mao invited Khrushchev to swim with him to discuss relations. However, Khrushchev couldn't actually swim and had to wear armbands to keep up with Mao. Safe to say, Khrushchev did not take kindly to this embarrassment.

THE SINO-SOVIET SPLIT

'The cult of the personality of Mao Tse-tung has reached absurd lengths and has become actual idolatry.'
Soviet newspaper Pravda on the Sino-Soviet Split, 1967

What was the Sino-Soviet split?

The Sino-Soviet split is the term given to the breakdown of political relations between the Soviet Union and China.

When did the Sino-Soviet split happen?

The split developed during the 1950s, but relations rapidly declined in 1960 and the split was formalised in 1962.

Why did the Sino-Soviet split happen?

The split developed due to 6 key reasons and events:

- Mao had a strong distrust of Stalin. After charging excessive amounts for Soviet weapons during the Korean War, Mao believed Stalin was out to weaken and subjugate China.
- With Khrushchev's 'Secret Speech' and criticism of Stalin, Mao felt his style of government and regime was also being criticised. However, after this point Mao Zedong Thought *(p.47)* did become a less important policy for the Politburo.
- Despite attempts to improve relations, during the Moscow Conference of 1958, China accused the Soviets of spying and betraying the communist movement.
- In April 1960, relations began to deteriorate significantly. Mao accused the Soviet Union of being revisionist and not true to Marxist communism. In return, Khrushchev criticised the Great Leap Forward *(p.43)*.
- Khrushchev then returned all Soviet advisers to China, which significantly impacted its economic development.
- Finally, in 1962, Mao publicly denounced Khrushchev as a coward for his role in the Cuban Missile Crisis. Khrushchev responded by claiming Mao and China were irresponsible and their policies would lead to war.

What were the outcomes of the Sino-Soviet split?

There were 2 notable outcomes for China following the Sino-Soviet split:

- Mao looked to improve relations with the USA and several meetings took place between Mao and Nixon. This led to a series of mutual agreements in terms of economic and cultural developments.
- China became more concerned about a possible attack from the USSR, and their nuclear weapons were now deterrents against the Soviet Union.

DID YOU KNOW?

Tit for tat...

Mao booked Khrushchev into an hotel with no air conditioning and in an area with plenty of mosquitos! This was in response to Mao's visit to Moscow, when Mao felt as if he had been forgotten about during his visit.

THE CULTURAL REVOLUTION

The Cultural Revolution aimed to restore China's purity to Marxist ideals by removing opposition and promoting loyalty to Mao. The cult of Mao was advanced during this period, with 750 million copies of The Little Red Book being distributed across China.

What was the Cultural Revolution?

The Cultural Revolution was an attempt to reassert Mao's authority in China, promote Mao Zedong Thought *(p.47)* and purge opposition.

When was the Cultural Revolution?

The movement lasted ten years, from 1966 until 1976.

Who led the Cultural Revolution?

The Cultural Revolution was launched by Mao and organised by the Central Cultural Revolution Group. However, there were a number of other key individuals involved in its implementation.

- Chen Boda of the CCRG (Central Cultural Revolution Group).
- Lin Biao of the People's Liberation Army (PLA).
- Jiang Qing (Mao's 4th wife).
- Kang Sheng (Secret Police).

Why did the Cultural Revolution happen?

There were a number of causes and motivations for the Cultural Revolution:

- Desire for permanent change. Mao was worried that old habits and ideas would return. By removing these influences, the hope was the changes made by the CCP *(p.22)* would become permanent.
- Involvement of the youth. Mao believed being involved in the struggle was key to loyalty, as seen with the Long March. He wanted to create conditions where the youth could become real revolutionaries.
- Removal of bureaucrats. Mao was worried government agencies were run by financially motivated individuals. Removing these people would ensure no return to the class system seen under the Qing dynasty.
- To remove internal CCP *(p.22)* opposition. Mao believed people were conspiring to remove him from power, mainly Liu Shaoqi and Deng Xiaoping *(p.57)*. This was his opportunity to remove the threat.
- To remove revisionists. These were people who didn't support the Marxist view of communism. Mao believed people were weakening the revolution by promoting non-Marxists features such as private trade.

What were the key features of the Cultural Revolution?

There were 6 key features of the Cultural Revolution:

- Mass Mobilisation of Youth. Mao encouraged the youth to rally and attack revisionists as well as the 'old' ideas of China. In one rally on 18th August, 1966, over a million people attended to hear Mao speak.
- Attacks on the Four Olds. Following the rallies, young people were encouraged to attack anything which was old. The movement defined four areas in particular; old habits, old ideas, old culture and old customs.
- The Red Guard. The youth joined together to form units to attack opponents of the Cultural Revolution. They took part in violent attacks and in Guangxi alone 67,000 people were killed as a result.
- The cult of Mao. During this period Mao became a symbol of worship and images of him appeared everywhere. His 'Little Red Book' was published for the PLA and it was used by the Red Guard to guide their behaviour.
- Education. The Red Guard also set about challenging intellectuals at schools and universities. By the end of 1966, all schools were closed so that the youth could take part in the Cultural Revolution.
- PLA. The PLA played an important role in controlling the revolution. When the Red Guard had spiralled out of control in 1968, the PLA (on Mao's orders) shut down the group's operations and purged it. Thousands were killed.

What areas were impacted by the Cultural Revolution?

7 key areas were impacted by the Cultural Revolution:
- Mao's political position.
- China's economic situation.
- Education.
- Family life.
- Health.
- Religion.
- Culture.

How was Mao's position impacted by the Cultural Revolution?

The Cultural Revolution strengthened Mao's position in 4 ways:
- Mao used the Red Guard to attack opposition throughout the government. By 1969, 60% of the national communist party's high-ranking officials had been removed. The figure was even higher for provincial and regional officials.
- Mao was also able to target high ranking CCP *(p.22)* officials. Liu Shaoqi was ousted as a traitor and imprisoned, where he died in 1969.
- Overall, Mao became significantly more powerful. He had the CCP *(p.22)* firmly under control and anyone who challenged him had been removed.
- However, the Cultural Revolution also made him even more paranoid that leading CCP *(p.22)* members were plotting against him. More isolated than ever and with declining health, Mao was rarely seen in public again.

How was the economy impacted by the Cultural Revolution?

The Cultural Revolution led to 5 significant declines in the Chinese economy during the years 1966-70:
- Replacements for those purged were ill-trained and unable to run successful businesses.
- Due to the movement of the Red Guard around China, transports for moving goods and materials became scarce. This led to a shortage of materials and an inability of factories to keep up with production.
- Between 1966-70, production fell by 13%. The production of raw materials such as steel, oil and coal also reduced by c.25%.
- Agriculture also suffered slightly with grain production down, which led to the introduction of rationing.
- After 1969, the economy began to recover as the Cultural Revolution began to settle. However, this had halted China's plan for rapid industrialisation.

How was education impacted by the Cultural Revolution?

There were 2 key outcomes of the Cultural Revolution on education:
- Schools were closed from 1966-70.

- By 1982, only 35% of the population had schooling until they were 12, with less than 1% of the population having a degree.

How was family impacted by the Cultural Revolution?
The family unit was weakened as one of the 'Four Olds'. With the Mountains campaign sending many youth away from their families, the traditional model soon disintegrated.

How was health impacted by the Cultural Revolution?
There were 2 impacts of the Cultural Revolution on health:
- Healthcare was badly affected as doctors showed their loyalty to the revolution by downing tools.
- There was a growth in 'barefoot doctors', who had rapid, yet limited medical training and worked in rural areas as part of the revolution. This did help improve healthcare for peasants but only for general conditions which did not need extensive treatment or resources.

How was religion impacted by the Cultural Revolution?
Religion was damaged by the revolution. It was seen as one of the 'Four Olds' and was prohibited. While the majority of priests were sent to be re-educated, some continued in secret and eventually religion returned.

How was culture impacted by the Cultural Revolution?
Censorship was introduced during the revolution to remove traditional Chinese culture. Artists were threatened with prison so produced nothing which could be deemed part of the 'Four Olds'. This left a huge void in Chinese culture during this period.

DID YOU KNOW?

Badges brought China's industry to a standstill!
So many badges of Mao were being produced that he had to order production to be stopped. China had run out of aluminium and could no longer produce aircraft!

THE 'UP TO THE MOUNTAINS AND DOWN TO THE MOUNTAINS' CAMPAIGN

Following the purge of the Red Guards, Mao was left with thousands of enthusiastic youths. Having them in urban areas posed a potential threat, so this campaign aimed to minimise it by sending them out to communes in the countryside.

What was the 'Up to the Mountains and Down to the Villages' campaign?
The 'Up to the Mountains and Down to the Villages' campaign encouraged young people to move to the country to learn the lifestyle of peasants.

When did the 'Up to the Mountains and Down to the Villages' campaign happen?
The campaign followed the purge of the Red Guards in 1968 and ran until the early 1970s.

Who took part in the 'Up to the Mountains and Down to the Villages' campaign?

The campaign was targeted at the youth, who had followed or supported the now-redundant Red Guard. It is estimated 17 million young people were involved in the campaign.

Why did the 'Up to the Mountains and Down to the Villages' campaign happen?

There were 4 main reasons Mao launched the campaign:

- To send the remaining Red Guards to remote areas, where less disruption and damage could be caused.
- To minimise unemployment levels in the cities.
- To increase control over the Red Guard, as the PLA had more communes in the countryside.
- To create a new revolutionary struggle and teach the youth about the peasantry.

What were the outcomes of the 'Up to the Mountains and Down to the Villages' campaign?

The policy was not an overwhelming success due to 2 main reasons:

- Young people did not enjoy peasant life. This experience made them question Mao's authority.
- The peasants showed some resistance to the scheme because it put more pressure on their food supply, by having to feed the Red Guard.

> **DID YOU KNOW?**
>
> **Being a revolutionary could be quite painful...**
> Healthcare professionals stopped issuing anaesthetics to revolutionaries during this period. They promoted the idea of revolutionaries accepting pain without any reaction as part of their own struggle.

THE GANG OF FOUR

With Mao's death, a power vacuum emerged and the Gang of Four looked to assert themselves as the group which would seize control. However, they didn't expect the appointment of Hua, who swiftly dealt with their potential threat.

What was the Gang of Four?

The Gang of Four was a group of 4 leading CCP *(p.22)* members, who joined together in order to assume power once Mao died.

Who were the Gang of Four?

There were 4 key members of the gang:

- Zhang Chunqiao, a leading member of the Politburo.
- Wang Hongwen, who had long-standing affiliations to the party, first as a peasant and then as a soldier. He was chosen as Mao's successor in 1973.
- Yao Wenyuan, an official within the Office of Propaganda.
- Jiang Qing, Mao's fourth wife and the leader of the Gang of Four. She led cultural reform during the Cultural Revolution *(p.53)*.

When did the Gang of Four operate?
The Gang of Four came together during the Cultural Revolution *(p.53)* and operated until they were arrested in October 1976.

What were the key events of the Gang of Four?
There were 5 key events which led to the downfall of the Gang of Four:
- Following Deng Xiaoping's *(p.57)* fall and Zhou Enlai's death, the Gang of Four believed they would assume power once Mao died.
- However, Mao appointed Hua Guofeng as premier of the PRC and the vice-chairman of the CCP *(p.22)* following Deng's removal.
- Mao died in September 1976 and the scramble to assume the leadership began. However, with Hua Guofeng's appointment, this now meant the Gang of Four had a leadership rival within the CCP *(p.22)*.
- The Gang of Four had limited support in the politburo and within the PLA. On the 6th October, 1976, Hua had the gang arrested on suspicion of various crimes.
- Between 1980-81, the Gang of Four faced trial for making several attempts to seize power from within the party and for their treatment of opponents. Jiang Qing was highlighted as a ringleader who carried out brutal attacks on the opposition during the Cultural Revolution *(p.53)*.

What were the outcomes of the Gang of Four's trial?
There were 4 key outcomes from the Gang of Four's trial:
- Jiang and Zhang received life sentences.
- This initially strengthened Hua's position within the CCP *(p.22)* as key opposition had been removed.
- However, due to the focus on the Gang of Four, Deng Xiaoping *(p.57)* was able to secure military support and consolidate his role in the party.
- In October 1978, Deng Xiaoping *(p.57)* was appointed paramount (supreme) leader of China.

DID YOU KNOW?

The Gang of Four's fame came from a play...well, from them banning one!

They became well known in 1965 after they banned Wu Han's play 'Hai Rui Dismissed from Office'. It was seen as damaging to values of the country as it promoted the story of Hai Rui, who openly criticised the emperor.

DENG XIAOPING

'It doesn't matter whether a cat is black or white, if it catches mice it is a good cat.'
Deng Xiaoping, 1961

Who was Deng Xiaoping?
Deng Xiaoping is most famously known for being the leader of China during the late 20th century.

When did Deng Xiaoping live?
Deng was born in 1904 and died in 1997.

Where was Deng Xiaoping born?

Deng was born in Guang'an, China.

What was Deng Xiaoping's role?

Deng's role changed over time. Following the Zunyi conference *(p.30)*, he was promoted and became a key figure in the CCP *(p.22)*. He would go on to rule China as paramount (supreme) leader from 1978 to 1989.

DID YOU KNOW?

Deng was a chain smoker!

Deng had his very own cigarettes, made just for him by Panda Cigarettes. He often offered these out when foreign visits were made to China.

ECONOMIC CHANGE UNDER DENG XIAOPING

'A fundamental contradiction does not exist between socialism and a market economy.'
Deng Xiaoping, 1985.

What economic changes happened under Deng Xiaoping?

There were a number of economic changes which took place under Deng. He believed in approaching the economy with a flexible mentality and changing traditional communist ideas if needed.

What were the aims of Deng Xiaoping's changes?

Deng had 3 main aims:
- He wanted to modernise China.
- Deng wanted to open up China to trade with the outside world.
- Foreign investment was to increase under Deng's leadership.

What changes did Deng Xiaoping make to agriculture?

Deng made 5 changes to the agricultural system:
- Communes were abolished and replaced with Xiangs (village or town).
- Each Xiang (village or town) had a quota which it had to meet and supply to the state.
- The surplus could then be sold for profit by the individual farmers.
- The new system was known as the 'household responsibility system'. It also permitted farmers to decide which crops to plant, allowing flexibility according to land and weather.
- The impact was huge and 98% of agricultural land was part of the system. Grain production saw a 144% growth during the years 1978-89. The programme was seen as a huge success.

What changes did Deng Xiaoping make to education?

Deng made 4 key educational reforms as he saw this as vital to the modernisation programme:
- University entry exams were introduced.
- Private universities were allowed and encouraged.
- Chinese students were encouraged to travel to the capitalist West for education.

- ✅ Research programmes and establishments were relaunched, which ended the repression caused by the Cultural Revolution *(p.53)*.

What changes did Deng Xiaoping make to industry?

Deng had a mixed approach to industry, keeping some of Mao's policies in place but also introducing others which led to the following 4 developments:

- ✅ State-owned enterprises remained but the freedom to set production targets and make profits was given to employees.
- ✅ He implemented an open-door policy, which encouraged businesses to produce quality goods which could be exported overseas.
- ✅ Special Economic Zones (SEZs) were set up in a number of coastal cities. These were areas where foreign investment was encouraged for both exports and home industries.
- ✅ These policies were a great success, with a 500% increase in export trade by 1990. Manufacturing output also increased by 34% from 1978 to 1989.

What changes did Deng Xiaoping make to privatisation?

Due to the industrial changes, China began moving towards a privatisation model and Deng introduced 2 key changes:

- ✅ Businesses, both in the Special Economic Zones on the coast, and inland, began to make profits.
- ✅ A rural version of the SEZ was the 'Town and Village Enterprise' system, which employed 100 million people by 1990.

DID YOU KNOW?

Deng may have found his inspiration abroad!

Deng spent 11 months in Moscow in the 1920s. He attended the Communist University of the Toilers of the East, which was a training school for communist leaders-to-be. Prior to this he spent 4 years in France.

BIRTH CONTROL

With a desire to improve quality of life in China, Deng Xiaoping introduced population control measures to ensure the country could support its population.

What was China's policy towards birth control?

China's policy towards birth control was conservative. They wanted to reduce the growing population and introduced the 'one-child' policy under the new marriage law *(p.41)*.

Why was the 'one-child' policy introduced?

The policy was introduced as China's population had rapidly grown to 974 million by 1979. The government was concerned it wouldn't be able to provide for the population if it continued to rise.

What were the key details of the 'one-child' policy?

There were 4 key details to the 'one-child' policy:

- ✅ Minimum ages for marriage were raised to 22 years old for men and 20 years old for women.
- ✅ Married couples were only allowed to have one child. If you had more, you would be fined.
- ✅ You had to apply for a permit in order to have a child.

- ☑ If you already had more than one child, the state could abort any further pregnancy or sterilise a woman to avoid more.

What were the outcomes of the 'one-child' policy?

There were 4 main outcomes from this policy:
- ☑ There was an increase in female infanticide.
- ☑ This led to a gender imbalance and, by 1985, only 100 females were born to every 114 males.
- ☑ The policy also had to be incentivised, with one-child families receiving better health care and education.
- ☑ Overall, the policy succeeded in slowing China's birth rate and the growth of its population.

DID YOU KNOW?

The 'one-child policy' only ended in October 2015.
The threshold was raised so families could have 2 children.

POLITICAL CHANGE UNDER DENG

Deng continued to uphold and promote Mao's political structure and values. With Deng coming to power, it was important for him to consolidate his support and he did this by driving economic changes, rather than political ones.

What political changes did Deng make?

Deng did not make any political changes. He wanted to keep the Marxist core of the party and continued to follow Mao Zedong Thought *(p.47)*.

What were the key ideas of Deng's political reforms?

Deng's political approach can be summed up by 4 key ideas:
- ☑ The CCP *(p.22)* would retain control of China.
- ☑ There would be only one political party, the CCP *(p.22)*.
- ☑ Free elections would not be held.
- ☑ Censorship would continue in order to quash any principle of free speech.

DID YOU KNOW?

Deng was relatively small, measuring around 5 feet in height.
On its own this isn't interesting, but height in China is now considered alongside education in job applications. In today's world, Deng's height could have put him at the bottom end of the social structure.

THE DEMOCRACY WALL MOVEMENT

'They had two main slogans: to overthrow the Communist Party and topple the socialist system. Their goal was to establish a bourgeois republic entirely dependent on the west.'
Deng Xiaoping, June 1989

What was the Democracy Wall Movement?
The Democracy Wall Movement, or the Democracy Movement, was a campaign for political reforms in order to continue the modernisation of China.

Who took part in the Democracy Wall Movement?
The movement was spearheaded by students and intellectuals.

When did the Democracy Wall Movement begin?
The movement began in 1979, following the arrest of an electrician named Wei Jingsheng's in 1978.

What were the key events of the Democracy Wall Movement?
In 1985, mass student protests began in Beijing which led to 2 further key demonstrations:
- Student demonstrations spread across the whole of China and by 1986, many universities saw similar protests.
- While these protests were crushed, the Democracy Movement would rise again in 1989 with protests at Tiananmen Square.

Why did the Democracy Wall Movement happen?
These protests broke out for 6 main reasons:
- Following Wei Jingsheng's arrest in 1978, protests emerged. Wei had posted an essay criticising Deng's approach towards democracy on a wall near Tiananmen Square.
- Initially, protests were over the arrest of Wei Jinsheng but also because of poor living conditions and high rents.
- Students and intellectuals who had experienced Europe and America had seen an alternate type of government. They wanted democracy so the party could represent the people and address their problems.
- There were also criticisms of the government. Economic issues such as unemployment were blamed on the CCP *(p.22)* as preferential treatment was being given to family and friends of members of the party.
- This also led to claims that the CCP *(p.22)* was suffering from corruption. The lack of free speech compounded this and many now wanted a voice. Students began to call for democracy for China.
- In response to calls for democracy, Deng tightened control even further by the increasing use of censorship and arrests. This addressed the 1986 protests, but the repression only led to further protests in 1989.

DID YOU KNOW?

Wei Jingsheng ended up in the USA!
After being arrested, Wei spent 18 years in Chinese prisons before being exiled to the USA in 1997.

TIANANMEN SQUARE

'This storm was bound to happen sooner or later. As determined by the international and domestic climate, it was bound to happen and was independent of man's will. It was just a matter of time and scale.'
Deng Xiaoping, June 1989

What were the Tiananmen Square Protests?
Tiananmen Square, or the Tiananmen Square Protests, were student-led protests against the government demanding more freedom for the people of China.

When did the Tiananmen Square Protests happen?
The protests started on the 15th April, 1989, and were crushed on 4th June, 1989.

Where did the Tiananmen Square Protests happen?
The protests took place in Tiananmen Square in Beijing.

Why did the Tiananmen Square Protests happen?
There were 4 important reasons for the Tiananmen Square Protests:
- Issues raised by the Democracy Movement had not disappeared. However, they came back to the forefront following the death of Hu Yaobang.
- Hu Yaobang was sacked as general secretary of the CCP *(p.22)* after expressing sympathy for the students. He died in April 1989.
- Following Hu Yaobang's death, students gathered in Tiananmen Square to mourn. They offered a petition to ask for greater freedoms in honour of Yaobang's death.
- The petition was rejected by Premier Li Peng. This inspired more students to travel to Tiananmen Square to protest. Students were also gathering support from other avenues of society, with transport officials allowing them free journeys.

What were the key events of the Tiananmen Square Protests?
There were 6 key events in the Tiananmen Square Protests:
- Following Yaobang's death, students began to gather on Tiananmen Square on 15th April, 1989. They petitioned Premier Li Peng to offer greater freedoms.
- Protests grew into sit-ins, fights with police forces, and hunger strikes. By May 1989, it is estimated 300 students were on hunger strike.
- Deng did not act and avoided the protests, as Gorbachev was visiting from the Soviet Union. On 19th May, once Gorbachev left, Deng declared martial law.
- However, the wider population of Beijing joined the protests, blocking roads and preventing military forces from accessing Tiananmen Square.
- The government deployed 350,000 PLA troops on 2nd June, 1989. On 3rd June, they announced they would clear the square 24 hours later.
- As announced, the PLA proceded to clear the square with soldiers and armoured vehicles. The protesters resisted and the PLA opened fire on them, causing heavy casualties. The square was eventually cleared.

What were the outcomes of the Tiananmen Square Protests?
There were 6 key outcomes from the Tiananmen Square Protests:
- Thousands of protestors were killed and wounded resisting the PLA.
- After the protest was crushed, anyone suspected of involvement was arrested and imprisoned. Any CCP *(p.22)* member who had shown sympathy to the protests was removed.

- Deng demonstrated his determination and willingness to defend the political status-quo. It was a powerful message to anyone who thought about rebelling against the CCP *(p.22)*.
- International reactions to the event was one of anger. The USA placed economic sanctions on China and the Soviet Union condemned the attacks.
- China continues to claim that the Tiananmen Square massacre was a legitimate attack by the government against revolutionaries.
- Tight censorship and control has continued even to this day.

DID YOU KNOW?

The images and videos of 'Tank Man' have become iconic.
The image of 'Tank Man' blocking incoming tanks in Tiananmen Square was named one of the '100 Photographs That Changed the World' in 2003. If you haven't seen it, you know what to do!

GLOSSARY

A

Abolish, Abolished - to stop something, or get rid of it.

Agricultural - relating to agriculture.

Agriculture - an umbrella term to do with farming, growing crops or raising animals.

Alliance - a union between groups or countries that benefits each member.

Allies - parties working together for a common objective, such as countries involved in a war. In both world wars, 'Allies' refers to those countries on the side of Great Britain.

Ambassador - someone, often a diplomat, who represents their state, country or organisation in a different setting or place.

Assassinate - to murder someone, usually an important figure, often for religious or political reasons.

Assembly - a meeting of a group of people, often as part of a country's government, to make decisions.

Autonomy - independence or self-government.

B

Bolshevik, Bolsheviks - was a Russian radical Marxist revolutionary group, founded by Vladimir Lenin and Alexander Bogdanov in 1903. A Bolshevik is someone who is a member of that party.

Bribe, Bribery, Bribes - to dishonestly persuade someone to do something for you in return for money or other inducements.

C

Campaign - a political movement to get something changed; in military terms, it refers to a series of operations to achieve a goal.

Casualties - people who have been injured or killed, such as during a war, accident or catastrophe.

Ceasefire - when the various sides involved in conflict agree to stop fighting.

Censorship - the control of information in the media by a government, whereby information considered obscene or unacceptable is suppressed.

Civilian - a non-military person.

Claim - someone's assertion of their right to something - for example, a claim to the throne.

Coalition, Coalitions - a temporary alliance, such as when a group of countries fights together.

Commissions - the collective term for several organisations set up by the League of Nations to solve global issues.

Commune - a place where a group of people live and work together and share resources.

Communism - the belief, based on the ideas of Karl Marx, that all people should be equal in society without government, money or private property. Everything is owned by by the people, and each person receives according to need.

Communist - a believer in communism.

Conference - a formal meeting to discuss common issues of interest or concern.

Conscription - mandatory enlistment of people into a state service, usually the military.

Conservative - someone who dislikes change and prefers traditional values. It can also refer to a member of the Conservative Party.

Consolidate - to strengthen a position, often politically, by bringing several things together into a more effective whole.

Conventional - in accordance with what is considered normal or generally accepted. In military terms, it refers to non-nuclear weapons.

Cooperate, Cooperation - to work together to achieve a common aim. Frequently used in relation to politics, economics or law.

Council - an advisory or administrative body set up to manage the affairs of a place or organisation. The Council of the League of Nations contained the organisation's most powerful members.

Culture - the ideas, customs, and social behaviour of a particular people or society.

Currency - an umbrella term for any form of legal tender, but most commonly referring to money.

D

Democracy - a political system where a population votes for its government on a regular basis. The word is Greek for 'the rule of people' or 'people power'.

Democratic - relating to or supporting the principles of democracy.

Deploy - to move military troops or equipment into position or a place so they are ready for action.

Deterrent - something that discourages an action or behaviour.

Dictator - a ruler with absolute power over a country, often acquired by force.

Dictatorship - a form of government where an individual or small group has total power, ruling without tolerance for other views or opposition.

Dictatorship of the Proletariat - the belief that, whilst the proletariat would eventually come to rule itself as proposed by Karl Marx, for now they were not ready, and required a 'dictator' to guide them until they were able to rule themselves.

E

Economic - relating to the economy; also used when justifying something in terms of profitability.

Economy - a country, state or region's position in terms of production and consumption of goods and services, and the supply of money.

GLOSSARY

Empire - a group of states or countries ruled over and controlled by a single monarch.

Estate, Estates - an extensive area of land, usually in the country and including a large house. It tends to be owned by one person, family or organisation.

Exile - to be banned from one's original country, usually as a punishment or for political reasons.

Export - to transport goods for sale to another country.

Extreme - furthest from the centre or any given point. If someone holds extreme views, they are not moderate and are considered radical.

F

Famine - a severe food shortage resulting in starvation and death, usually the result of bad harvests.

Fascism - an extreme right-wing belief system based around racism and national pride. It was created by the Italian dictator, Benito Mussolini, and later adopted by Adolf Hitler.

Free elections - elections in which voters are free to vote without interference.

Front - in war, the area where fighting is taking place.

G

Guerrilla tactics, Guerrilla warfare - a way of fighting that typically involves hit-and-run style tactics.

Guerrillas - groups of small, independent fighters usually involved in a war against larger, regular military forces.

H

Harvest - the process of gathering and collecting crops.

Heavy industry - the manufacture of large and/or heavy items in bulk, or industries which involve large and heavy equipment and/or facilities. Examples are the iron, coal, steel and electricity industries.

I

Ideology - a set of ideas and ideals, particularly around political ideas or economic policy, often shared by a group of people.

Imperial, Imperialisation, Imperialism, Imperialist - is the practice or policy of taking possession of, and extending political and economic control over other areas or territories. Imperialism always requires the use of military, political or economic power by a stronger nation over that of a weaker one. An imperialist is someone who supports or practices imperialism and imperial relates to a system of empire, for example the British Empire.

Independence, Independent - to be free of control, often meaning by another country, allowing the people of a nation the ability to govern themselves.

Industrial - related to industry, manufacturing and/or production.

Industrialisation, Industrialise, Industrialised - the process of developing industry in a country or region where previously there was little or none.

Industry - the part of the economy concerned with turning raw materials into into manufactured goods, for example making furniture from wood.

Inflation - the general increase in the prices of goods which means money does not buy as much as it used to.

Integrate - to bring people or groups with specific characteristics or needs into equal participation with others; to merge one thing with another to form a single entity.

Intellectuals - people with a high intellect who engage in critical thinking and reading, research, writing, and self-reflection about society.

L

Legitimacy, Legitimate - accepted by law or conforming to the rules; can be defended as valid.

M

Martyr - someone who willingly dies for or is killed due to their beliefs, usually religious.

Mass - an act of worship in the Catholic Church.

Massacre - the deliberate and brutal slaughter of many people.

Middle class - refers to the socio-economic group which includes people who are educated and have professional jobs, such as teachers or lawyers.

Military force - the use of armed forces.

Minister - a senior member of government, usually responsible for a particular area such as education or finance.

Mobilisation - the action of a country getting ready for war by preparing and organising its armed forces.

Modernise - to update something to make it suitable for modern times, often by using modern equipment or modern ideas.

Mutiny - a rebellion or revolt, in particular by soldiers or sailors against their commanding officers.

N

Nationalisation - the transfer of control or ownership of a sector of industry, such as banking or rail, from the private sector to the state.

Nationalism, Nationalist, Nationalistic - identifying with your own nation and supporting its interests, often to the detriment or exclusion of other nations.

O

Occupation - the action, state or period when somewhere is taken over and occupied by a military force.

Offensive - another way of saying an attack or campaign.

GLOSSARY

P

Peasant - a poor farmer.

Population - the number of people who live in a specified place.

Poverty - the state of being extremely poor.

President - the elected head of state of a republic.

Prevent, Preventative, Preventive - steps taken to stop something from happening.

Production - a term used to describe how much of something is made, for example saying a factory has a high production rate.

Profit - generally refers to financial gain; the amount of money made after deducting buying, operating or production costs.

Propaganda - biased information aimed at persuading people to think a certain way.

Province, Provinces - part of an empire or a country denoting areas that have been divided for administrative purposes.

Purged, Purging - abrupt and often violent removal of a group of people from a place or organisation; medically, to make someone sick or induce diarrhoea as a treatment to rid them of illness.

R

Radical, Radicalism - people who want complete or extensive change, usually politically or socially.

Rallies, Rally - a political event with speakers and a crowd, designed to increase support for a politician, political party or an idea.

Rationing - limiting goods that are in high demand and short supply.

Rebellion - armed resistance against a government or leader, or resistance to other authority or control.

Rebels - people who rise in opposition or armed resistance against an established government or leader.

Reform, Reforming - change, usually in order to improve an institution or practice.

Reparations - payments made by the defeated countries in a war to the victors to help pay for the cost of and damage from the fighting.

Repress, Repression - politically, to prevent something or control people by by force.

Republic - a state or country run by elected representatives and an elected/nominated president. There is no monarch.

Revolution - the forced overthrow of a government or social system by its own people.

S

Sabotage - to deliberately destroy, damage or obstruct, especially to gain a political or military advantage.

Sanctions - actions taken against states who break international laws, such as a refusal to trade with them or supply necessary commodities.

Self-determination, Self-determined - in politics, the process where a nation decides its own statehood and whether it will rule itself rather than be part of a larger empire.

Sino - is a a reference to China or something relating to China. It is a prefix which is used instead of China.

Socialism - a political and economic system where most resources, such as factories and businesses, are owned by the state or workers with the aim of achieving greater equality between rich and poor.

Soviet - an elected workers' council at local, regional or national level in the former Soviet Union. It can also be a reference to the Soviet Union or the USSR.

Standard of living - level of wealth and goods available to an individual or group.

State, States - an area of land or a territory ruled by one government.

Sterilisation, Sterilise - to clean something so it is free of bacteria; also refers to a medical procedure that prevents a person from being able to reproduce.

Strategy - a plan of action outlining how a goal will be achieved.

Strike - a refusal by employees to work as a form of protest, usually to bring about change in their working conditions. It puts pressure on their employer, who cannot run the business without workers.

Successor - someone who succeeds the previous person, such as a leader who takes over the role from the previous holder.

T

Tactic - a strategy or method of achieving a goal.

Territories, Territory - an area of land under the control of a ruler/country.

The crown, The throne - phrases used to represent royal power. For example, if someone 'seizes the throne' it means they have taken control. Can also refer to physical objects.

INDEX

1

1911 revolution in China - *17*

A

Agrarian Reform Law - *40*

B

Battle of Huaihai - *39*
Boxer Uprising - *15*

C

Changes under Deng Xiaoping - *58*
Chiang Kai-shek - *21*
China in 1900s - *14*
China in early 1900s - *14*
China's First Five Year Plan - *43*
China's policy towards birth control - *59*
Chinese Civil War - *38*
Chinese Collectivisation - *42*
Chinese Communist Party - *22*
Chinese Great Famine, The - *45*
Cultural Revolution - *53*

D

Democracy Wall Movement, The - *61*
Deng Xiaoping - *57*
Deng's Political Reforms - *60*

E

Extermination campaigns - *26*

F

First United Front - *23*
Five-anti Campaign - *49*

G

Gang of Four - *56*
Great Leap Forward - *43*
Guomindang - *22*

H

Hundred Flowers Campaign - *50*

J

Japanese War - *36*
Japanese invasion of China - *35*
Jiangxi Soviet - *27*

L

Long March, The - *29*

M

Mao Zedong - *31*
Mao Zedong Thought - *47*
Mao's political changes - *47*
Marriage Law - *41*
May Fourth movement - *19*
Mukden incident - *27*

N

Northern Expedition - *24*

P

Policy towards women 1950-1962 - *45*

S

Self-strengthening reforms - *16*
Shanghai Massacres - *25*
Sino-Soviet relations between 1949-62 - *51*
Sino-Soviet split - *52*
Sun Yat-sen - *20*

T

Thought Reform - *48*
Three-anti Campaign, 1951. - *49*
Tiananmen Square Protests - *62*

U

Up to the Mountains and Down to the Villages Campaign - *55*

W

Warlords Era - *18*

X

Xian Incident - *34*

INDEX

Y

Yanan Soviet - *32*

Z

Zunyi Conference - *30*

Milton Keynes UK
Ingram Content Group UK Ltd.
UKHW050219090424
440832UK00005B/38